TOPICS

HEALTHY MOLAR__3
COMMONLY USED DENTAL RADIOGRAPHS_5
RESTORATION/FILLING___6
ROOT CANAL TREATMENT_8
STAGES OF CARIES_10
CROWN/CAP___11
WHY SHOULD WE REPLACE MISSING TEETH_14
BRIDGE TO REPLACE MISSING TEETH_15
DENTAL IMPLANTS_16
DENTAL POST & CORE_20
PERIODONTAL CARE_21
SENSITIVITY_23
INTER DENTAL BONE LOSS_24
BONE GRAFTING, SOCKET PRESERVATION_26
EXTRACTION,WISDOM TOOTH_30
WHY STRAIGHT TEETH ARE REQUIRED?_31
ORTHODONTICS, BRACES,ALIGNERS_33
TEETH WHITENING, VENEERS,COMPOSITE_38
SEMI FIX PROSTHESIS_41
REMOVABLE DENTURES_42
IMPORTANCE OF PRIMARY(MILK) TEETH_43
BRUSHING FOR KIDS_44
PREVENTIVE CARE
MOUTH GATEWAY OF HUMAN BODY_49
PULPOTOMY,PULPECTOMY_51
HABBITS,SPACE MAINTAINERS_52
TRAUMA,ATTRISION_54
CARIES SPREAD FROM MARGIN_57
CERAMIC CROWN CHIP,CRACK,DENTAL INFECTION_58
PAINKILLERS FOR DENTAL PAIN? THINK TWICE_61

SHORT, SIMPLE, AND BASIC CONCEPTS ARE EXPLAINED USING PICTURES

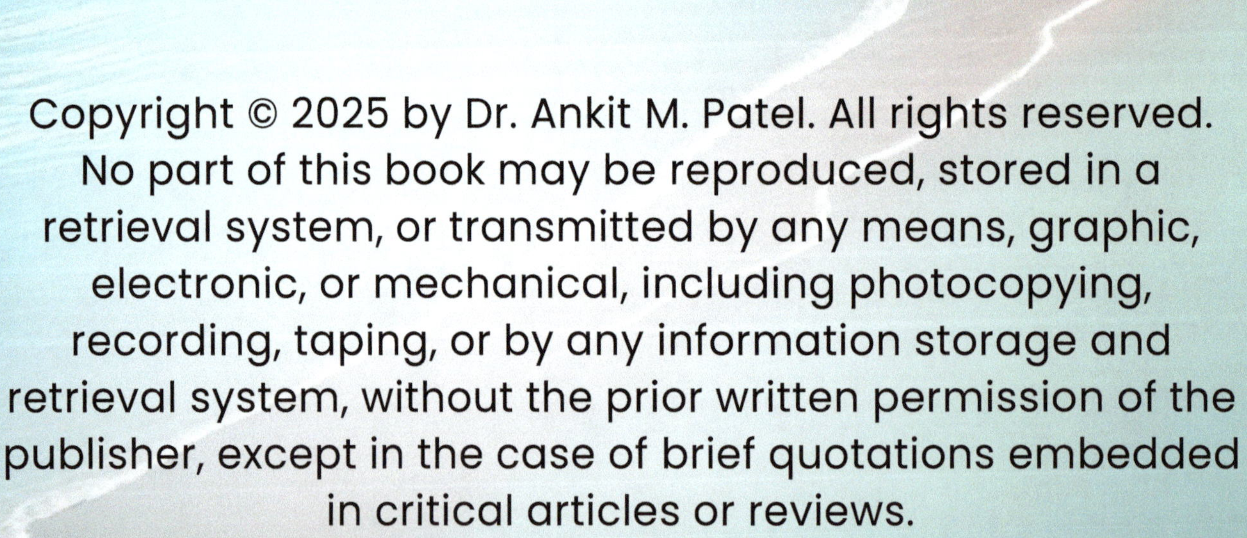

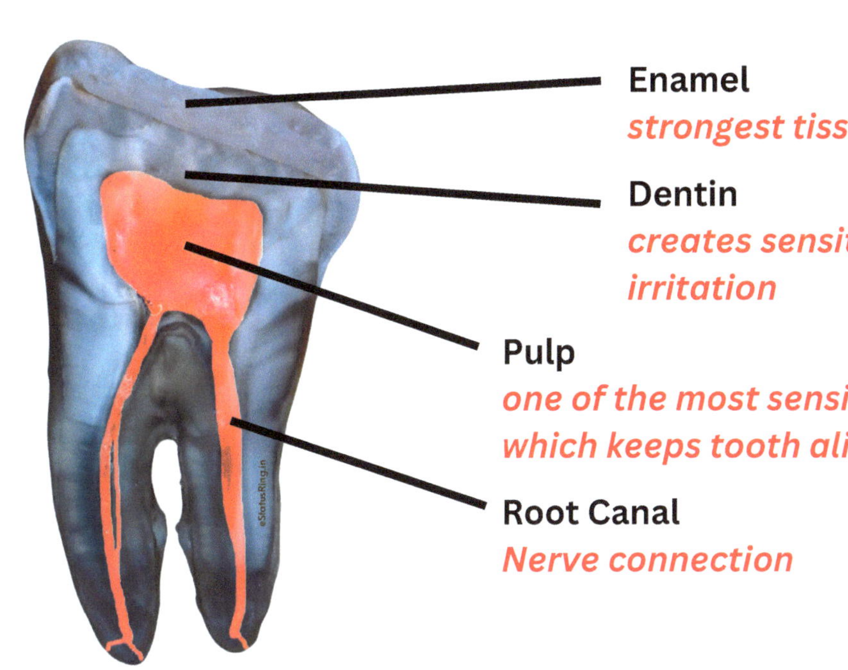

HEALTHY MOLAR TOOTH

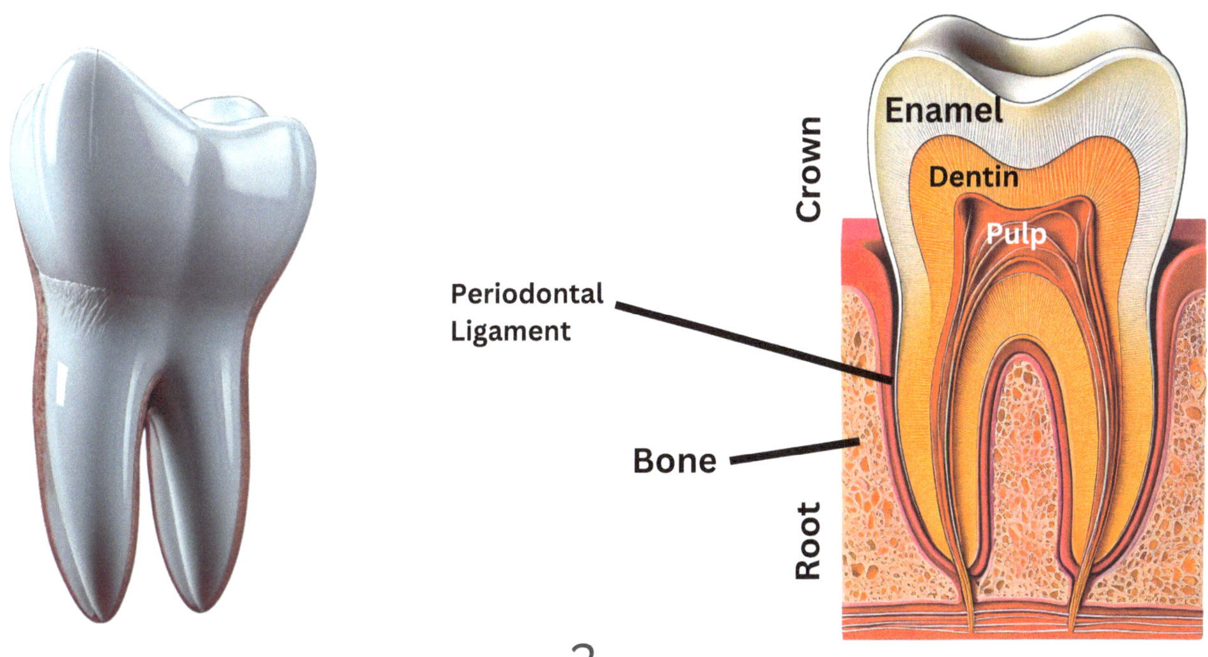

3

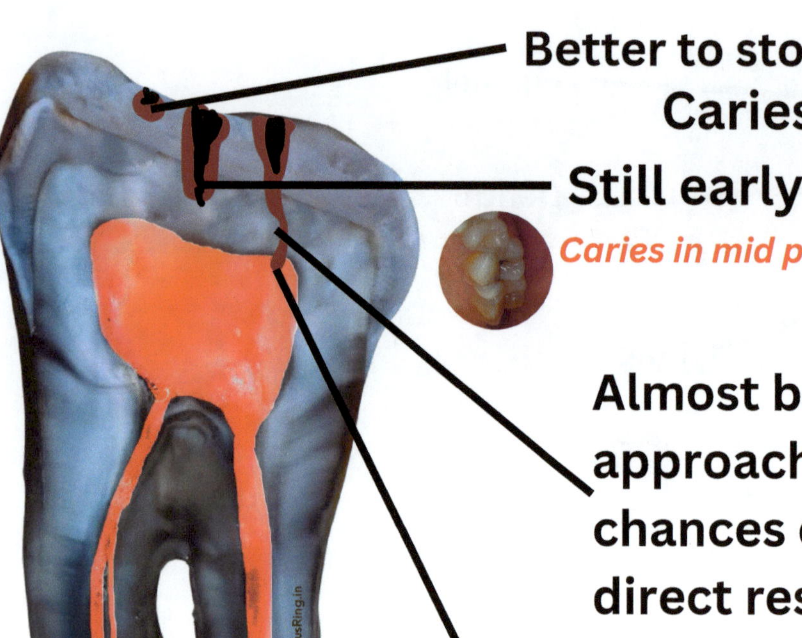

Better to stop here if started
Caries in enamel

Still early to stop here

Caries in mid part of dentine layer

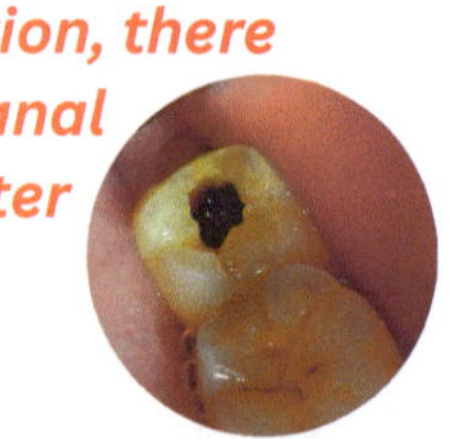

Almost borderline caries approaching pulp, less chances of survive with direct restoration

Based on clinical situation, there may be need for root canal treatment, during or after Restoration procedure

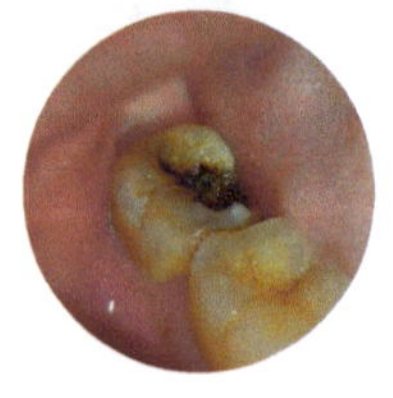

Pulpotomy/pulpectomy
More chance towards Root Canal Treatment

IT's in your hand where you want to stop
Because caries may progress without pain
Visit your dentist once or twice a year

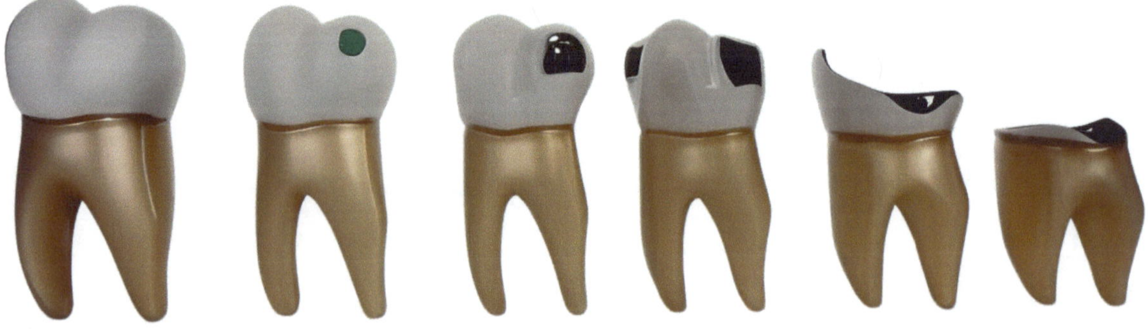

COMMONLY USED DENTAL DIAGNOSTIC
Radiographs

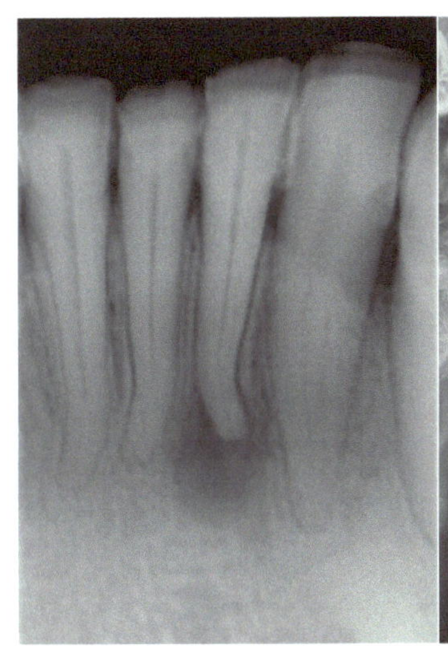

iopa xray

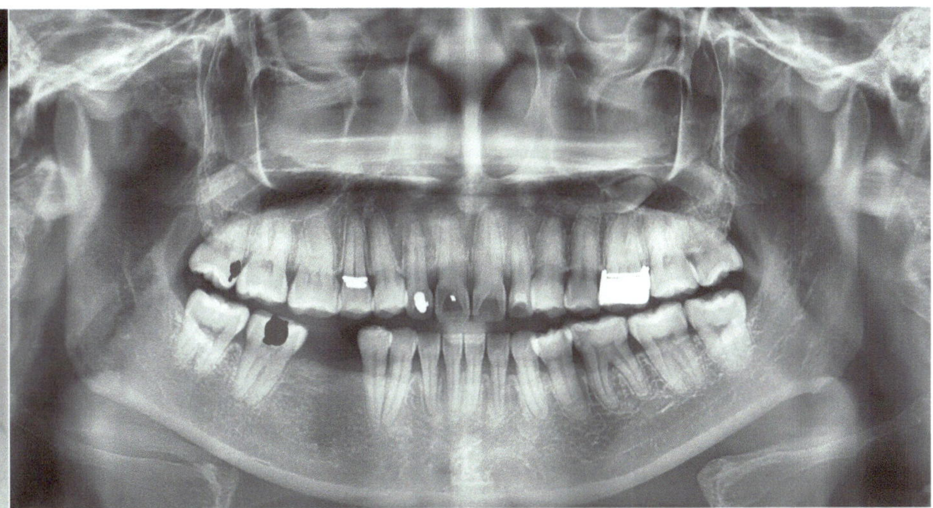

OPG xray

Bitewing

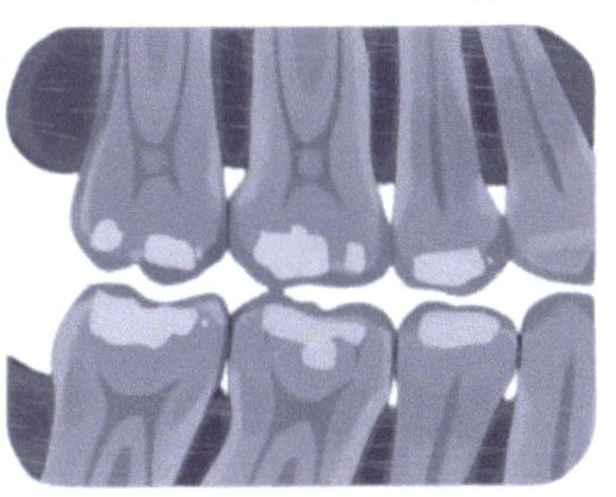

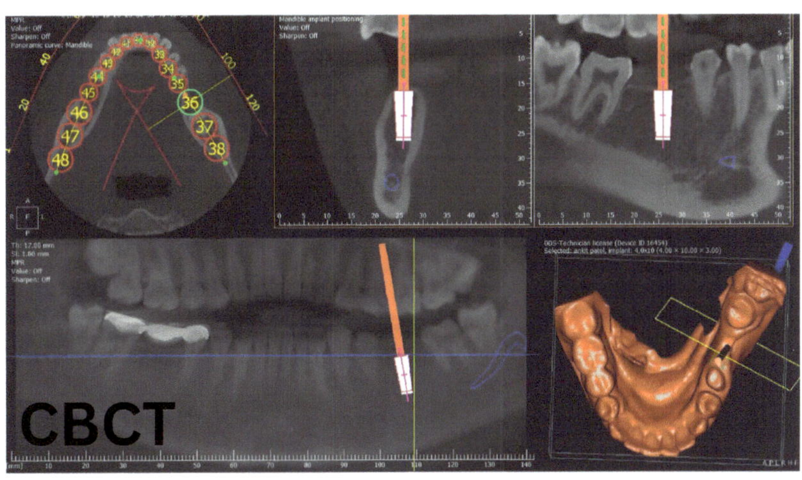

CBCT

FILLING RESTORATION

FOR PREVENTION OF CARIES SPREAD

Caries are painless at initial stage, it is better to stop early by fillings/restorations. its easy to find it on regular routine 6 month check-up some times x-rays helps more.

Frequently taken analgesics medication for headache, fever in recent month plays an important role in hiding signs and symptoms of dental pain/caries spread in few cases sensitivity or pain may present. Usually Composite, GIC, Silver amalgam etc are used as restoration material.

EARLY RESTORATIONS SAVES TIME , MONEY AND TEETH

IF LEFT UNTREATED IT MAY SPREAD MORE

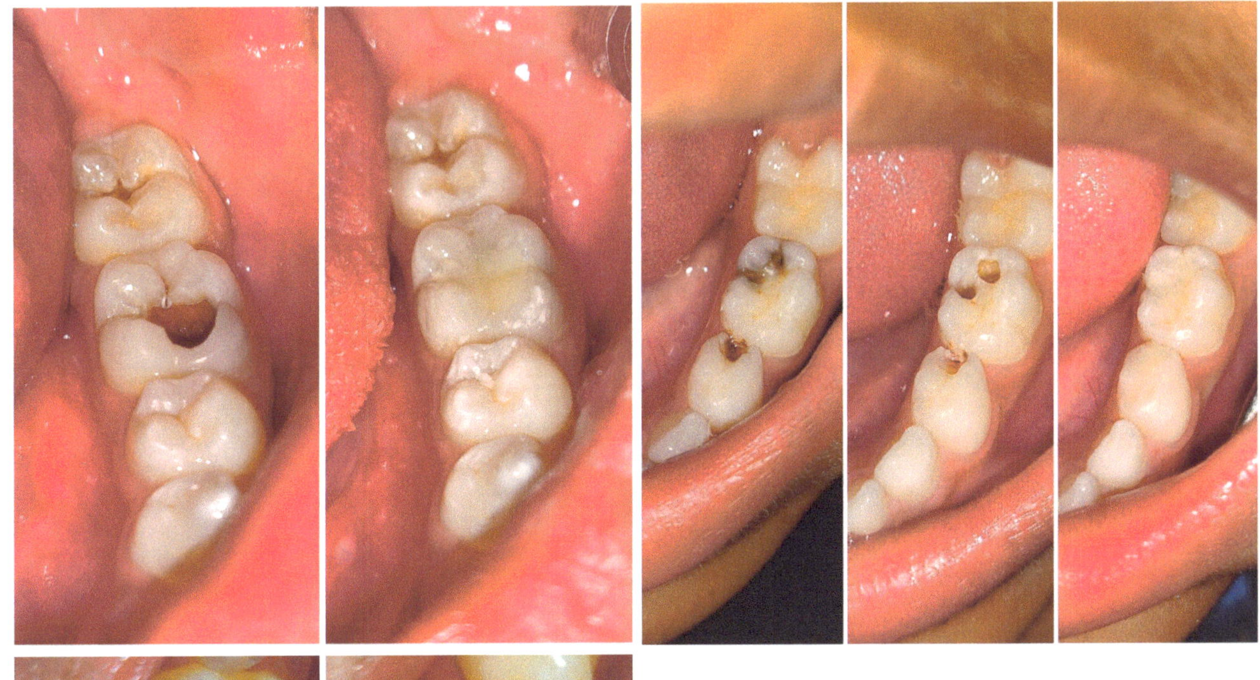

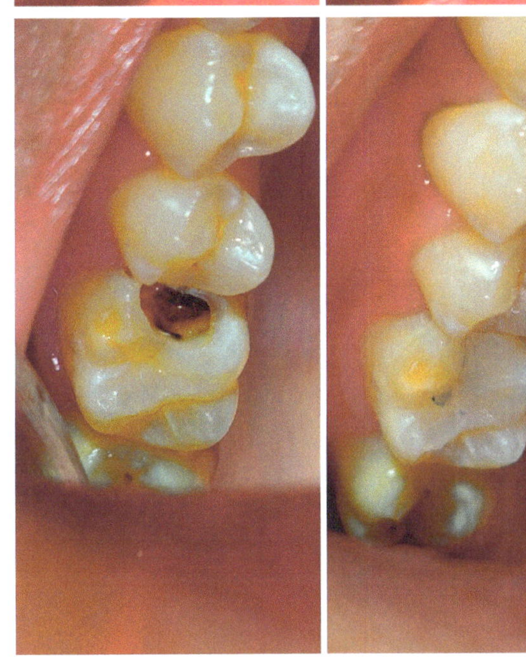

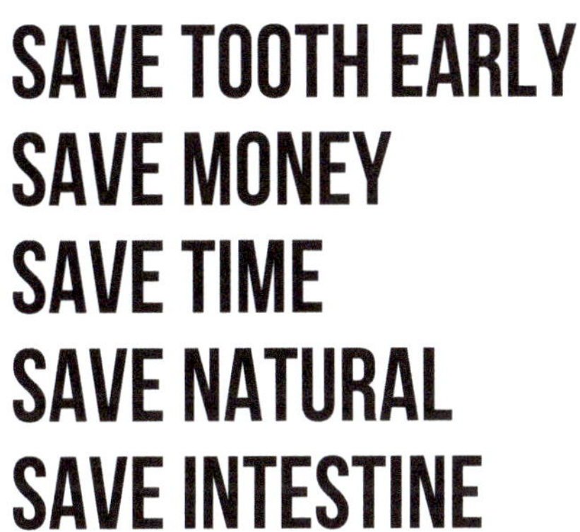

SAVE TOOTH EARLY
SAVE MONEY
SAVE TIME
SAVE NATURAL
SAVE INTESTINE

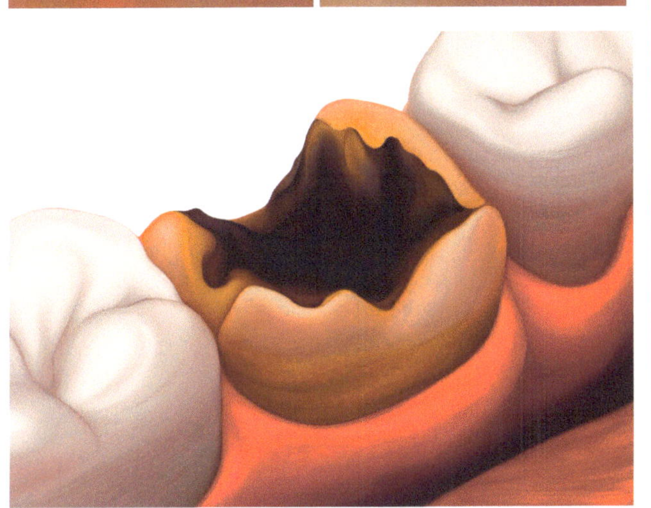

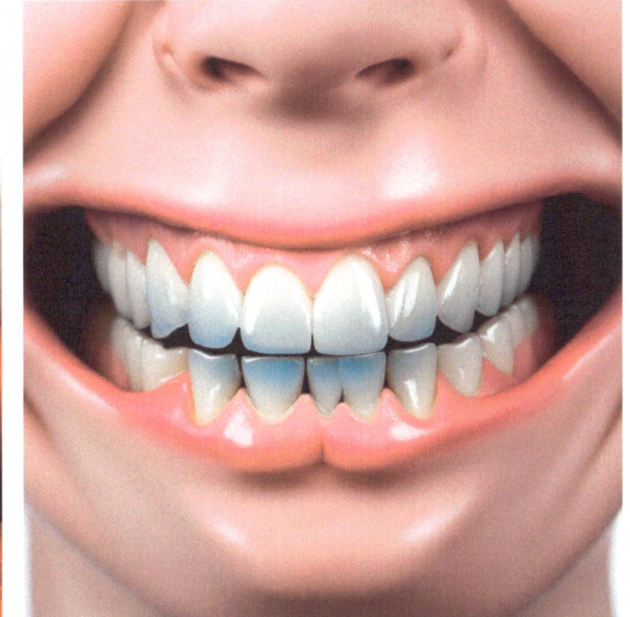

ROOT CANAL TREATMENT

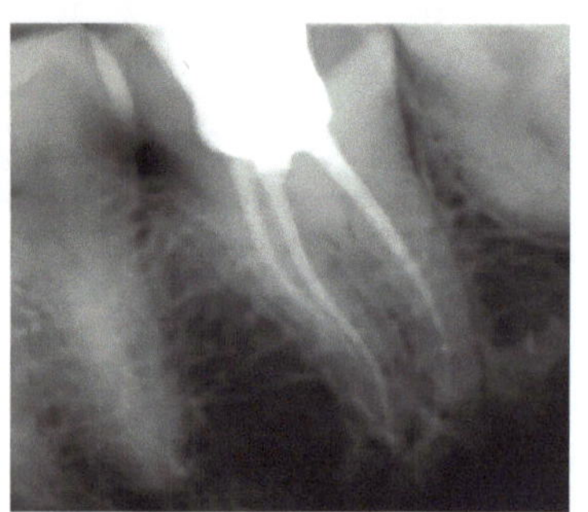

TO REDUCE PAIN & SAVE THE TOOTH

with or without asnaesthesia removal of caries and removal of infected pulp, Cleaning & filling is done inside canal after symptoms subsides tooth is restored.

its root canal therapy, mostly painless procedure depending on severity of lesion, tooth canal anatomy and position also matters patient should keep passions during this therapy it may take time to subside the toothach. Gutta percha material cones are filled in the canals and than tooth cavity is filled with restorative material.

DUE TO SOME CIRCUMSTANCES IF ROOT CANAL TREATMENT DOESN'T SOLVE THE PROBLEM RE-ROOT CANAL OR EXTRACTION ARE OPTIONS.

ROOT CANAL TREATMENT

	DEEP CARIES	WORKING LENGTH/FILING	GP CONE	POST RCF RESTORATION	CROWN TO PROTECT

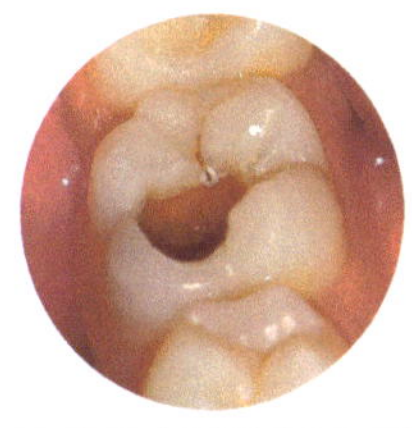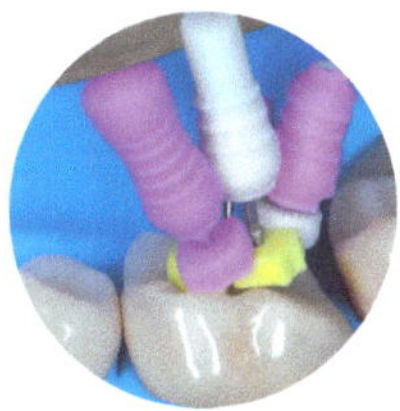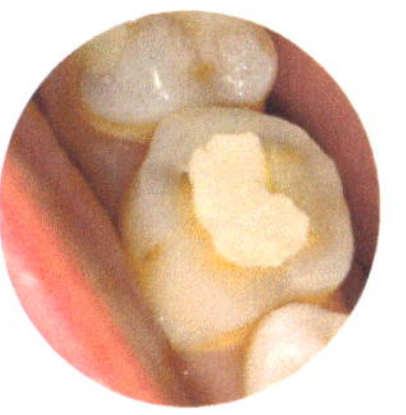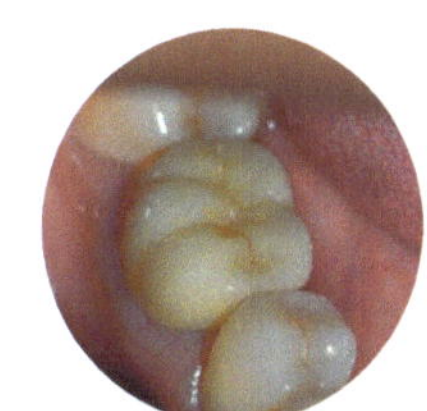

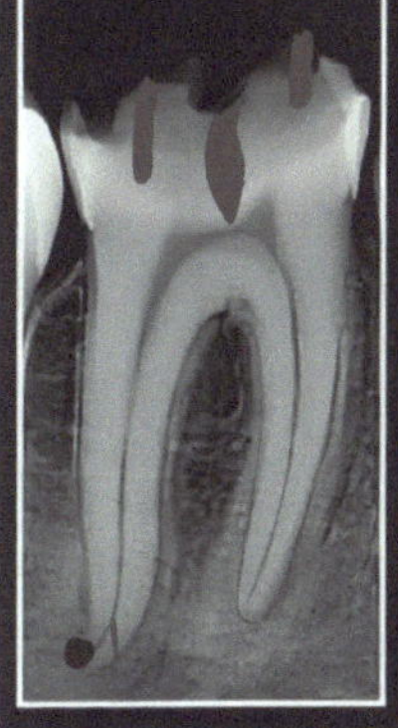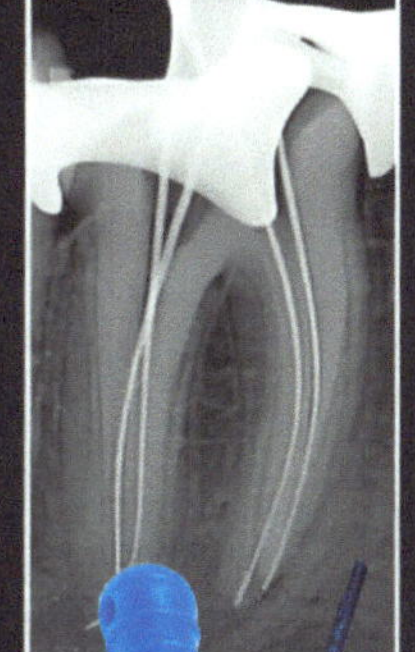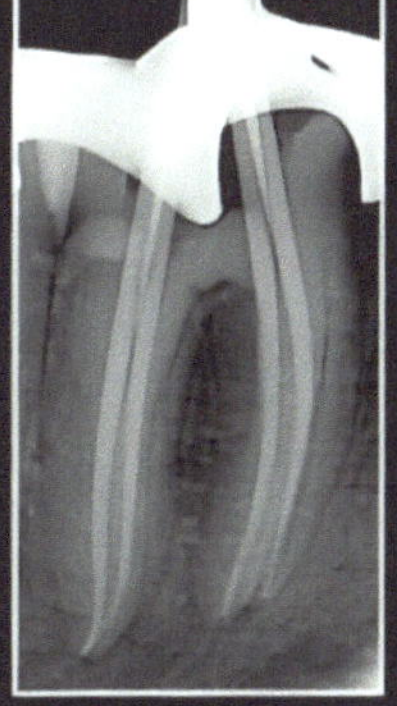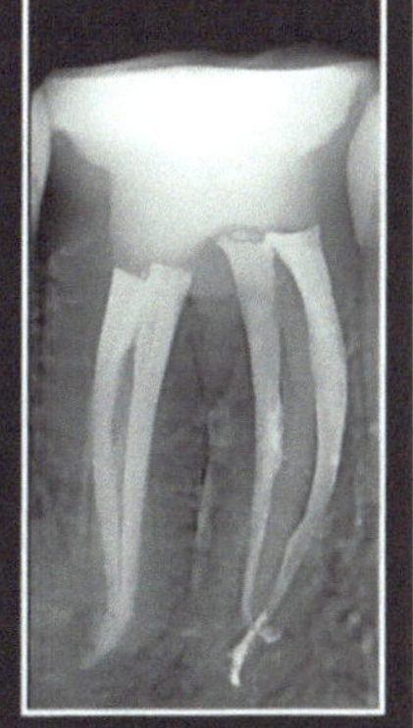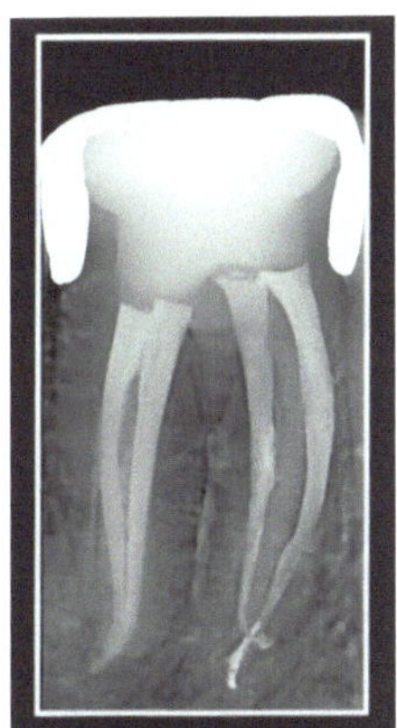

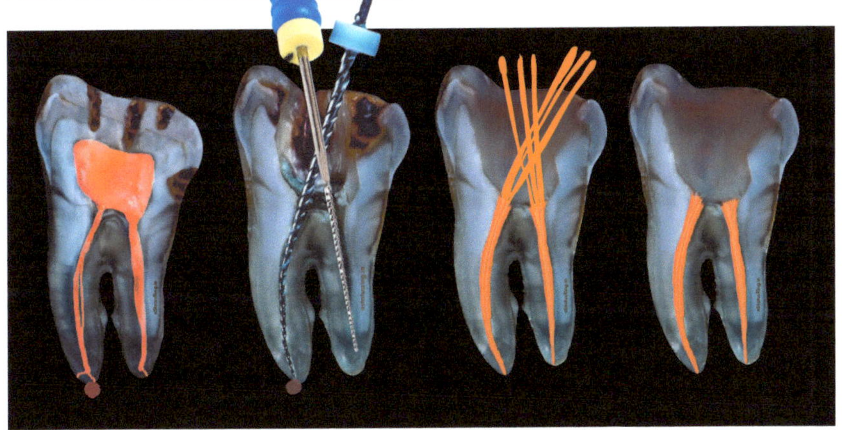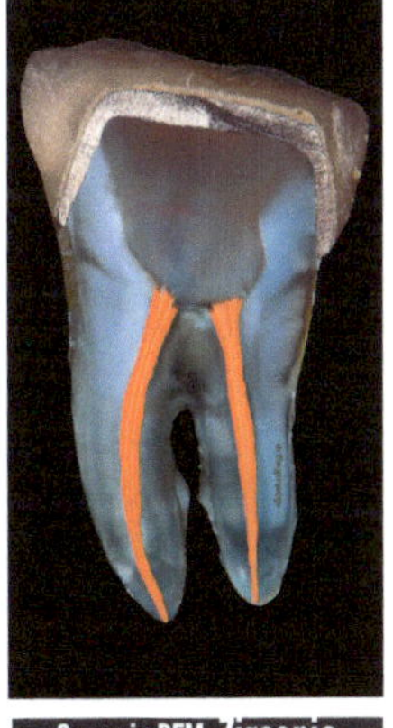

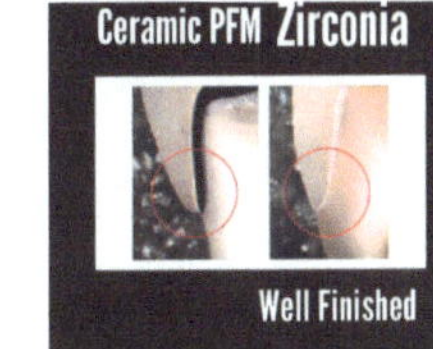

www.StatusRing.in

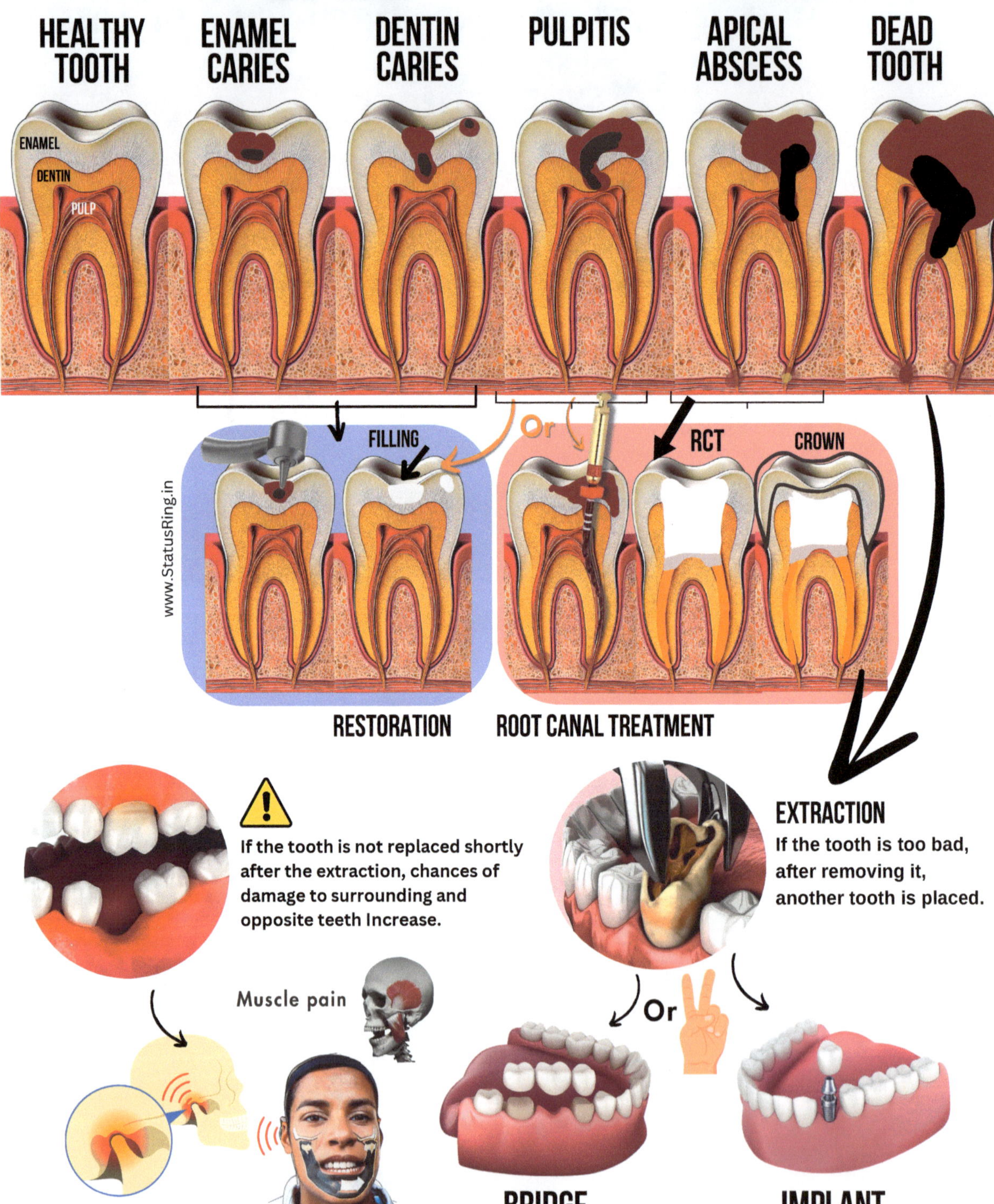

STAGES OF DENTAL CARIES
AND ITS CONSEQUENCES
DEEP CARIES
HEALTHY TOOTH
ENAMEL CARIES
DENTIN CARIES
PULPITIS
APICAL ABSCESS
DEAD TOOTH
ENAMEL
DENTIN
PULP
www.StatusRing.in
FILLING
Or
RCT
CROWN
RESTORATION
ROOT CANAL TREATMENT
EXTRACTION
If the tooth is too bad, after removing it, another tooth is placed.
If the tooth is not replaced shortly after the extraction, chances of damage to surrounding and opposite teeth Increase.
Muscle pain
Or
BRIDGE
IMPLANT
TMJoint Problems
Bite shifting causes jaw joint problems, headache earache

CROWN TO PROTECT TEETH/FILLING

IN SOME CASES CROWNS ARE NOT RECOMMENDED TO SAVE TOOTH STRUCTURE OR TO ALLOW ERUPTION OF ADJESANT TOOTH

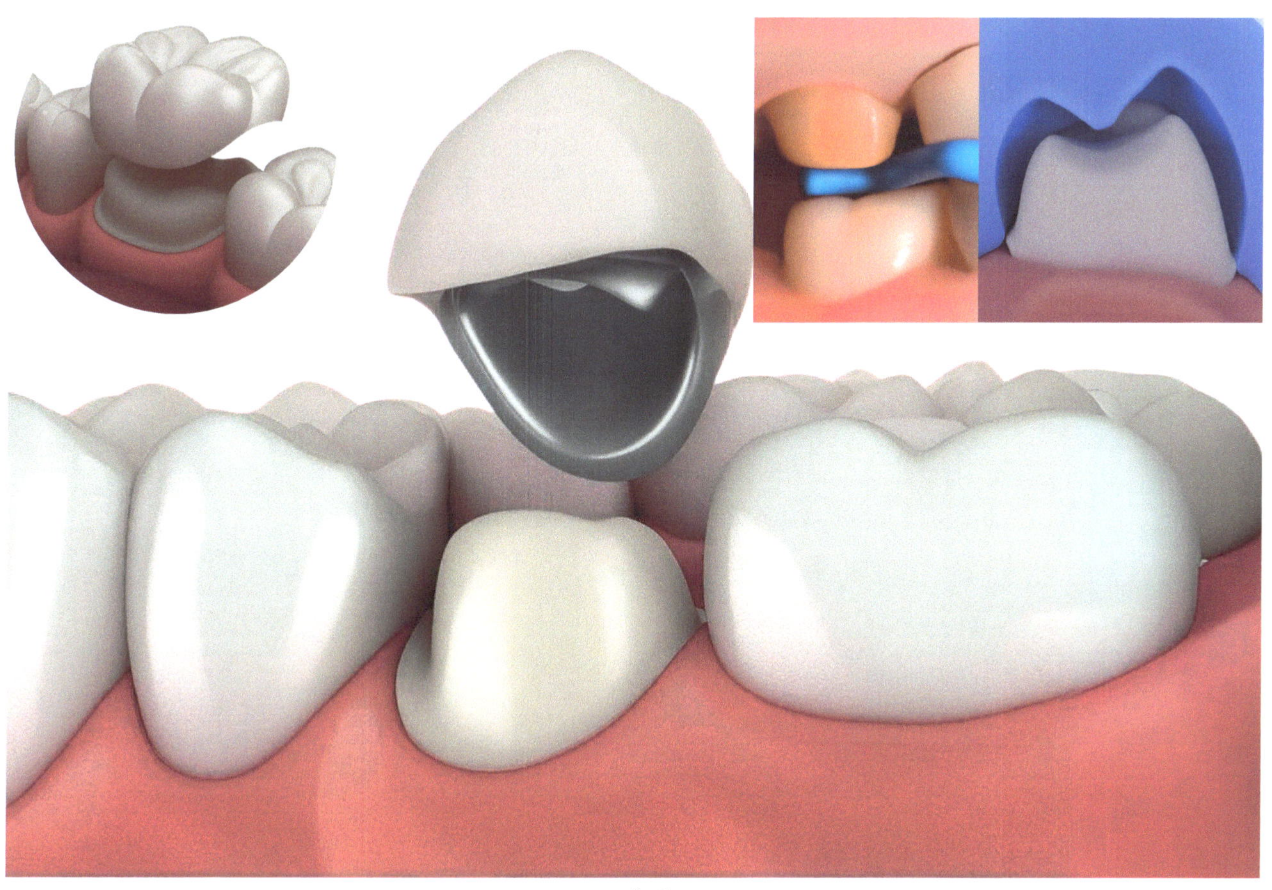

Prosthetic options to save tooth structure

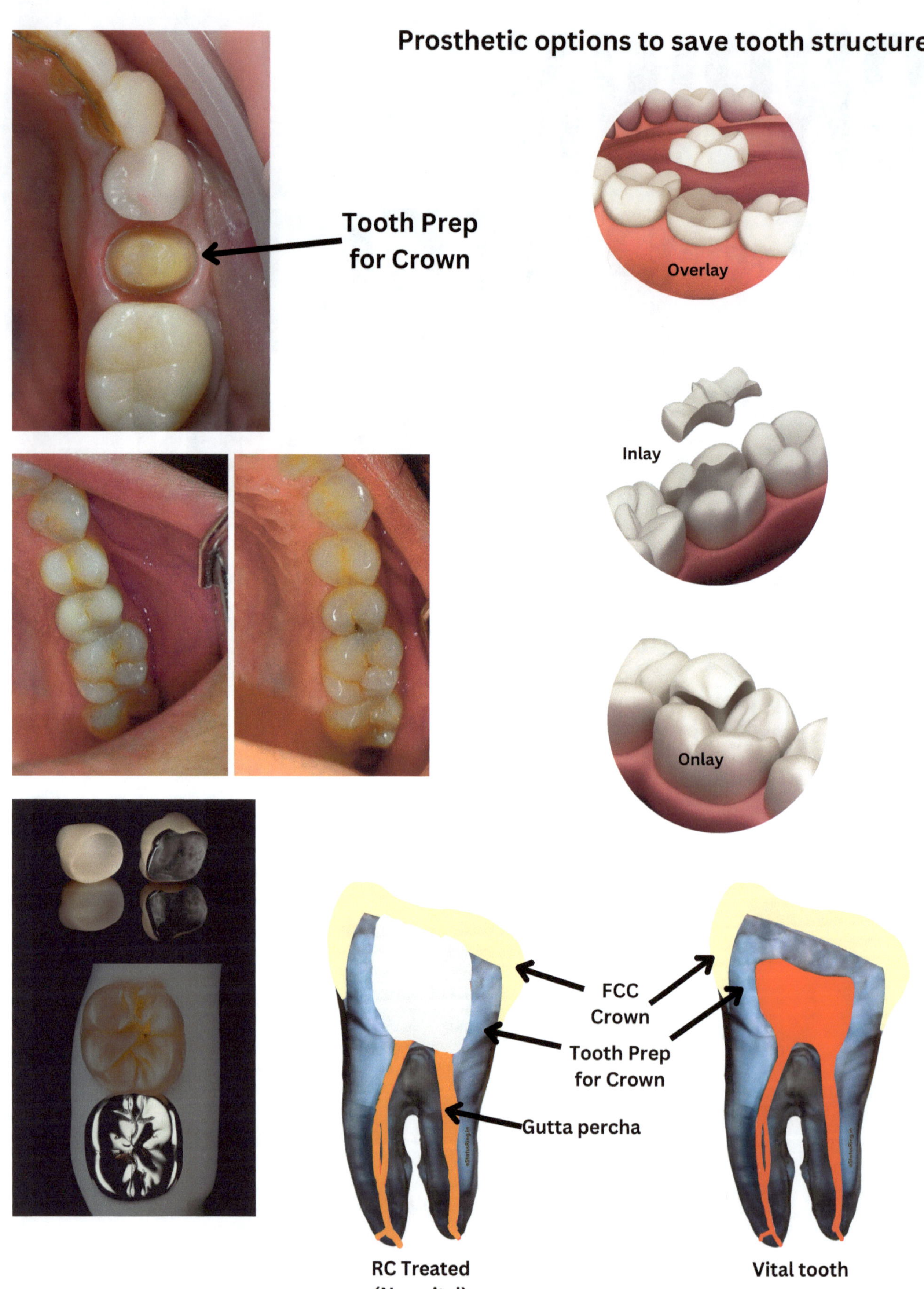

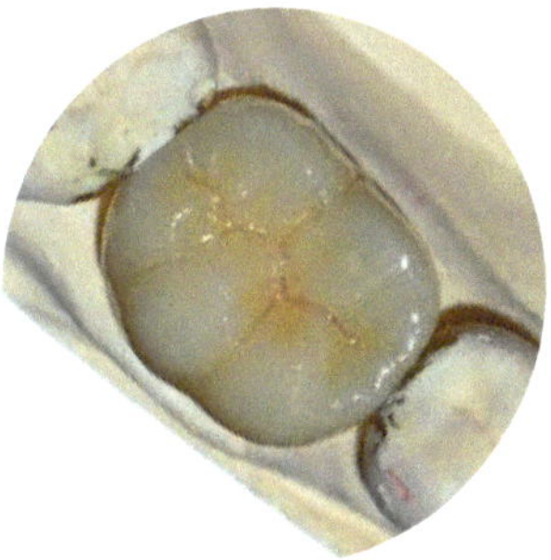

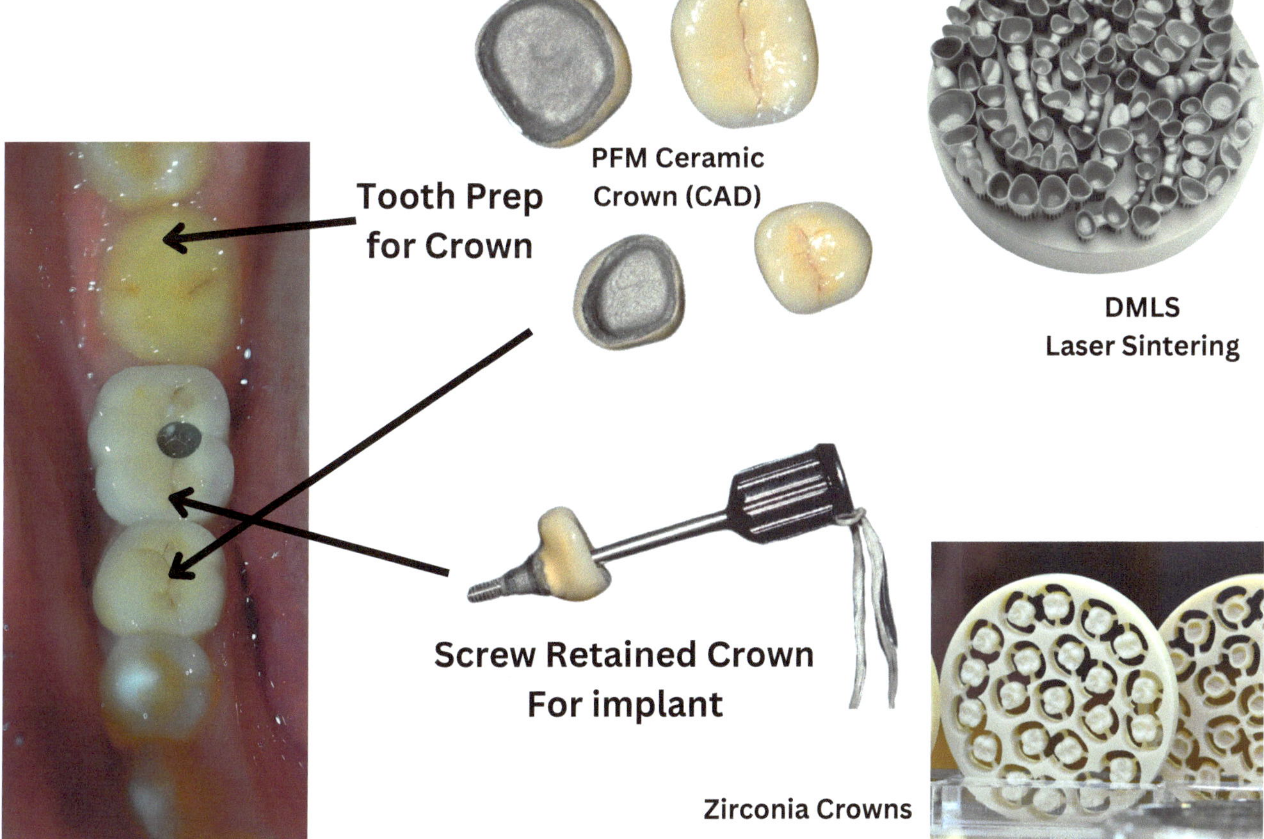

Zirconia Crown
(Layered)

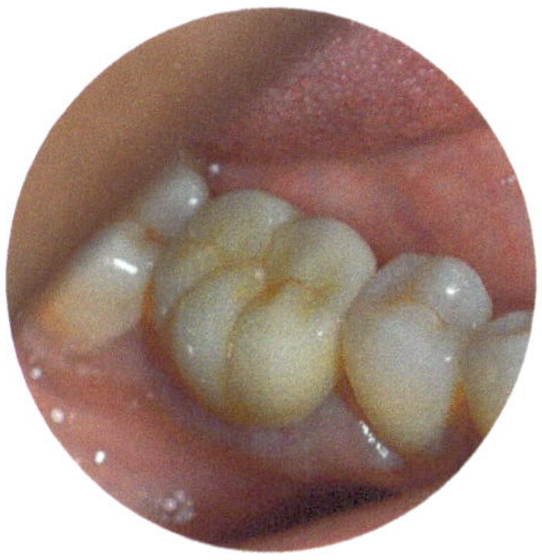

PFM Ceramic
Crown (CAD)

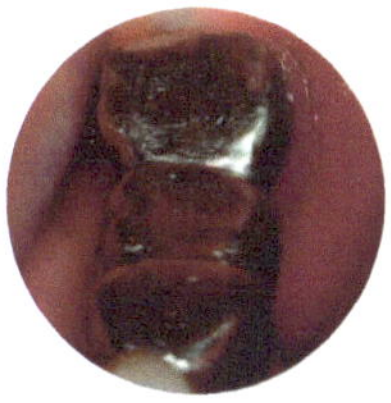

Metal Crown 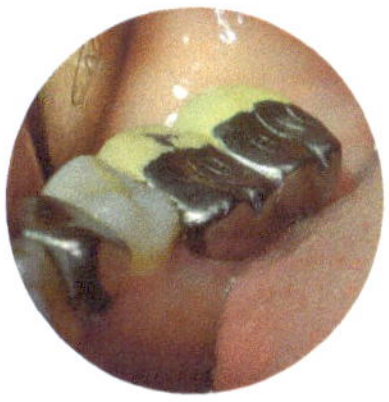   Ceramic Fused 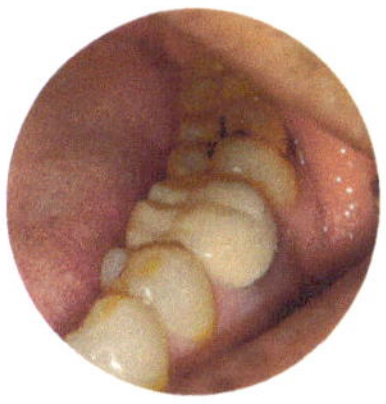   Ceramic PFM

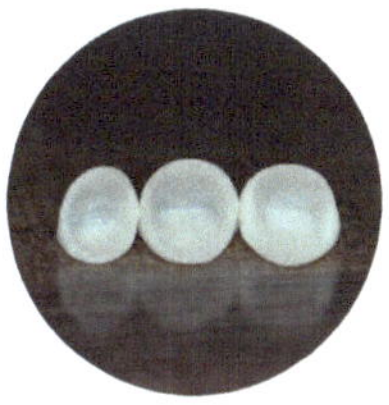

(CAD/CAM) MILLING IS
A DIGITAL PROCESS
THAT USES A MILLING
MACHINE TO CREATE
DENTAL PROSTHETICS
WITH PRECISION

Emax Crown

Tooth Prep
for Crown

PFM Ceramic
Crown (CAD)

DMLS
Laser Sintering

Screw Retained Crown
For implant

Zirconia Crowns

WHY SHOULD WE REPLACE MISSING TEETH?

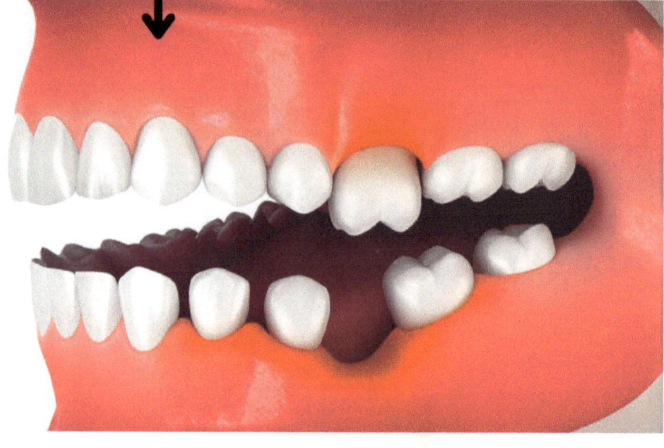

Supraeruption
sensitivity from cervical
food accumulation and caries
@proximal surfaces
traumatic and shifting bite

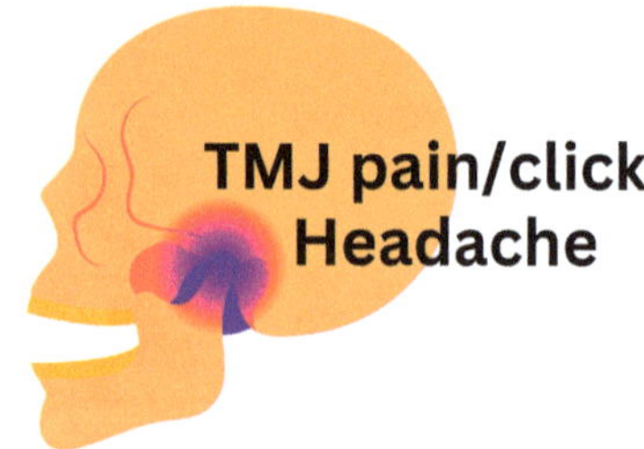

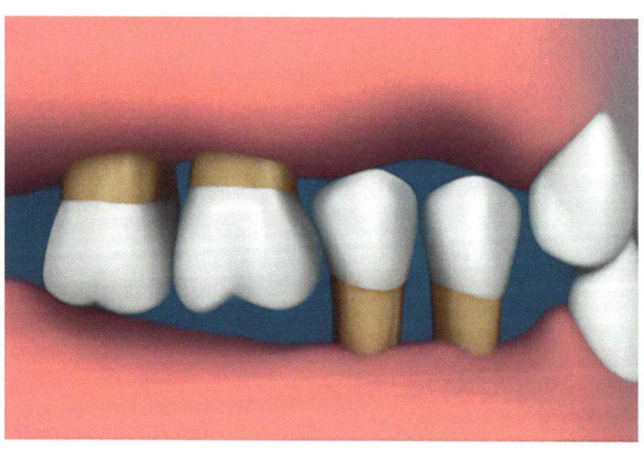

1. Prevent shifting of teeth
2. Restore chewing ability
3. Aesthetics
4. Prevent bone loss
5. Maintain facial shape

when all teeth are lost or removed

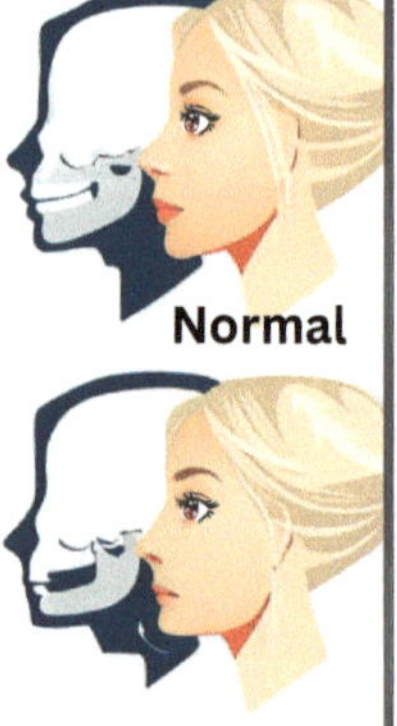

BRIDGE TO REPLACE MISSING TEETH

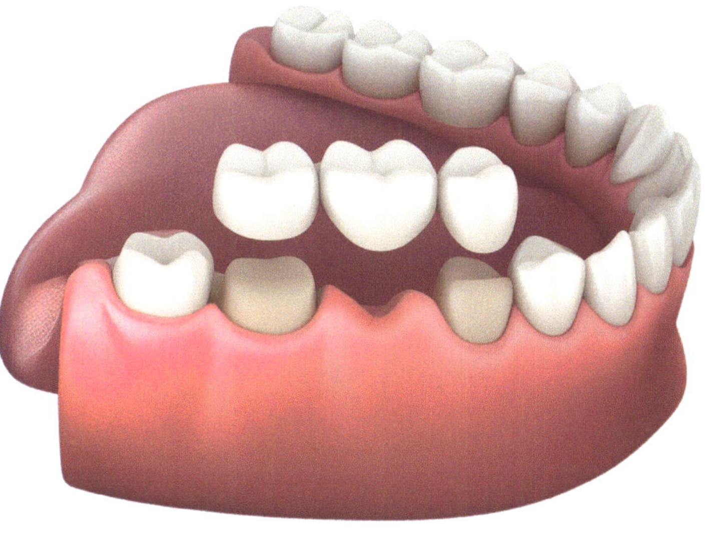

USING SUPPORT OF NREARBY GOOD HEALTHY TEETH
FASTER ,LESS INVESIVE ,CHEAPER THAN IMPLANT

POST OPERATIVE SENSITIVITY IS POSSIBLE
SOME TIME INTENTIONAL ROOT CANAL TREATMENT IS REQUIRED

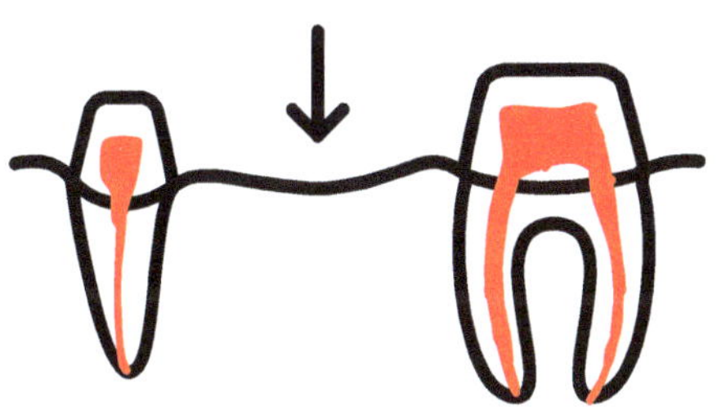

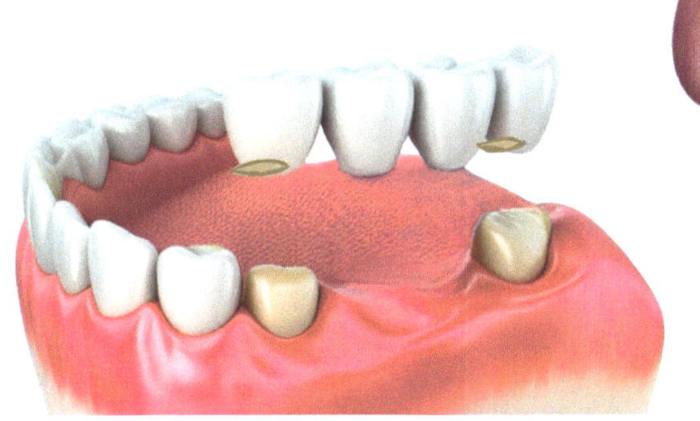

DENTAL IMPLANT

TO REPLACE MISSING TEETH

NOT USING SUPPORT OF NEARBY GOOD HEALTHY TEETH
SO WE CAN AVOID UNNECESSARY DAMAGE OF NEARBY TEETH

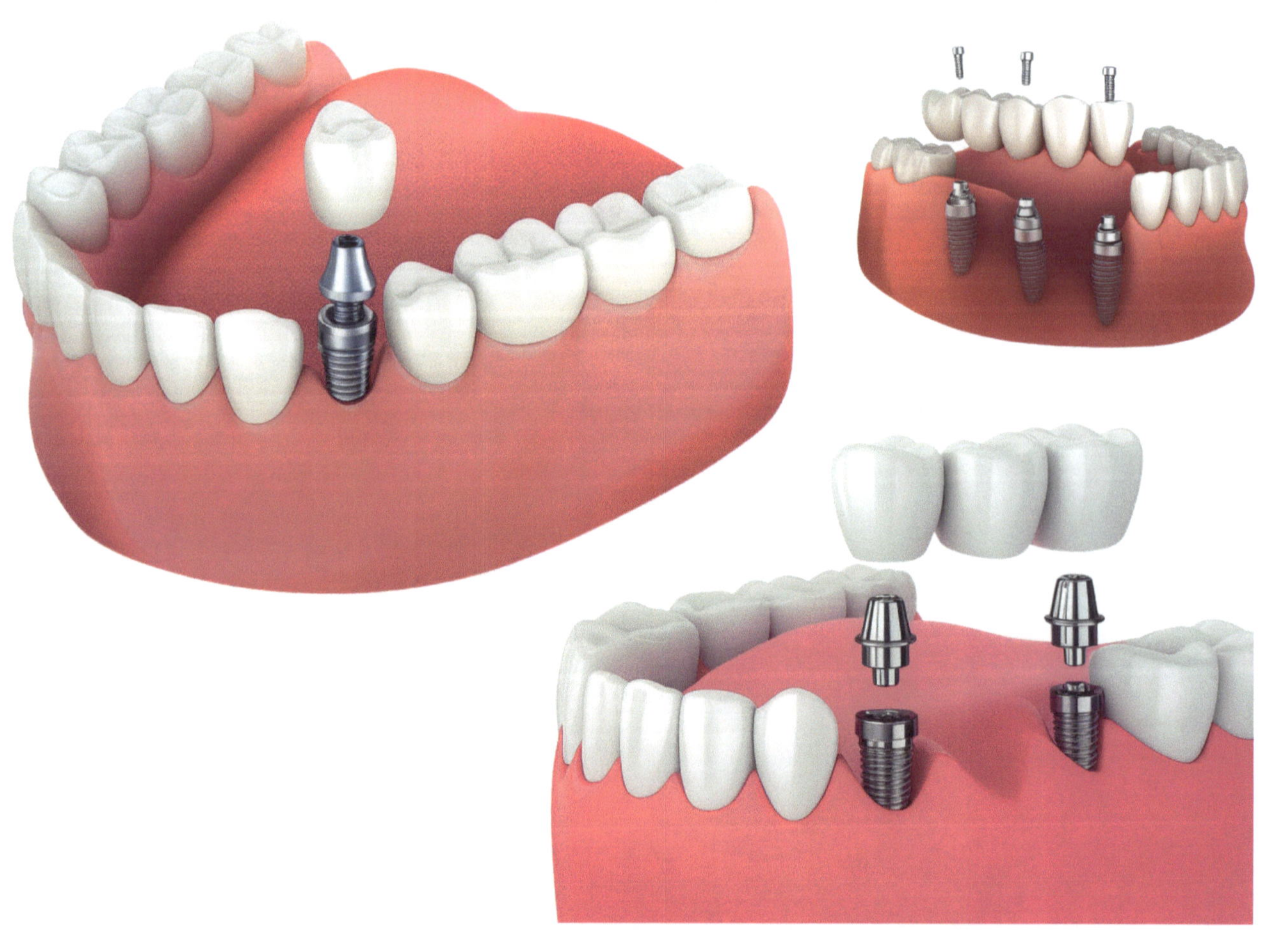

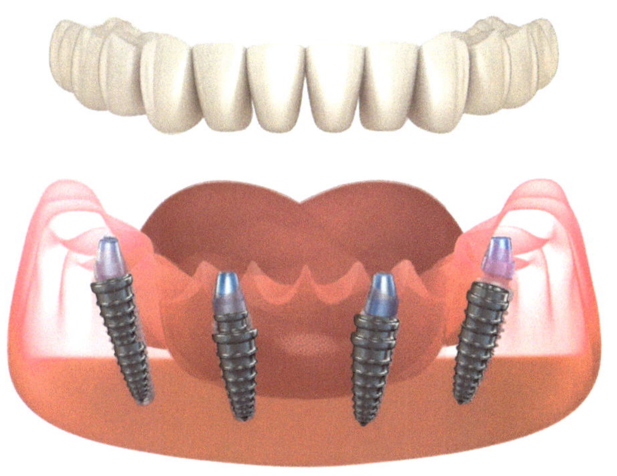

ALL ON 4

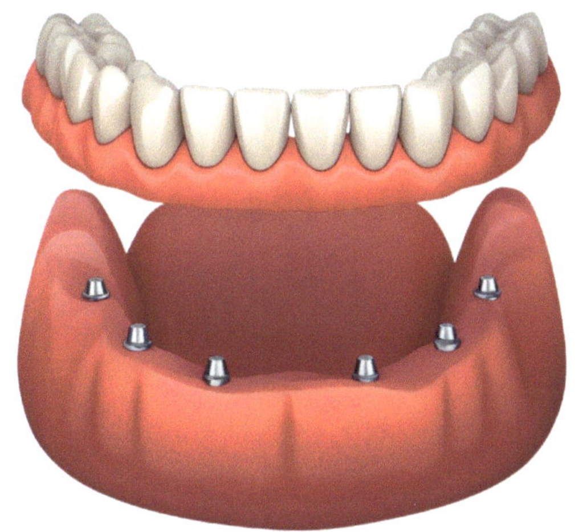

HYBRID PROSTHESIS

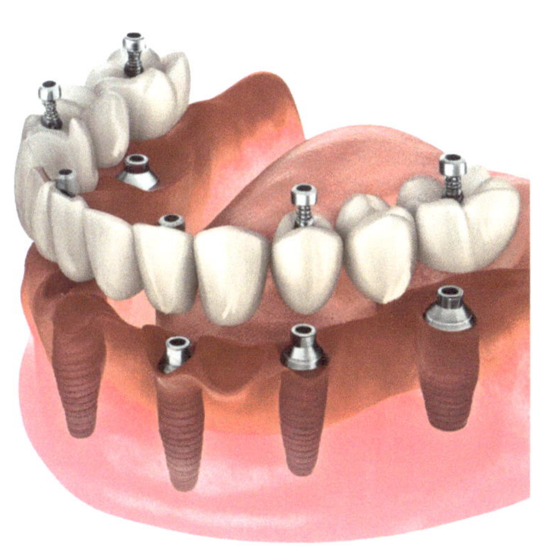

SCREW RETAINED

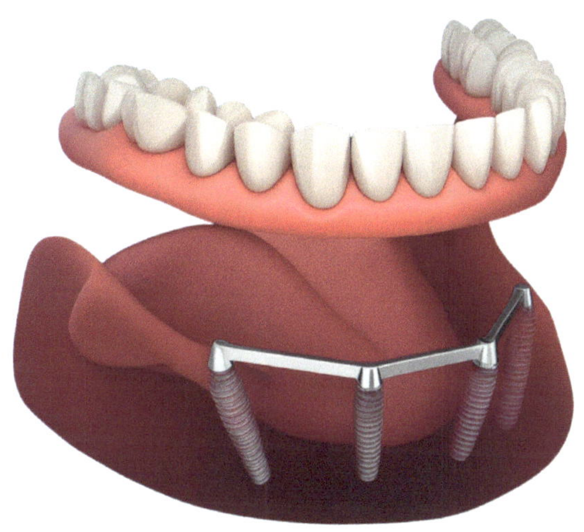

**BAR SUPPORTED DENTAL
IMPLANT PROSTHESIS**

DENTAL IMPLANTS

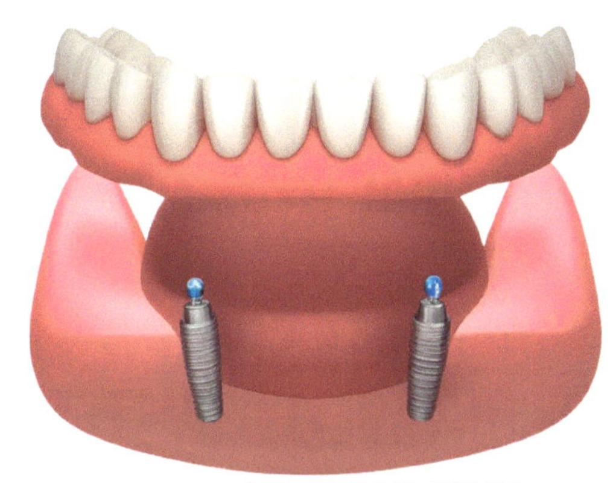

BALL ATTACHMENT

COMMON CHALLANGES IN DENTAL IMPLANTS

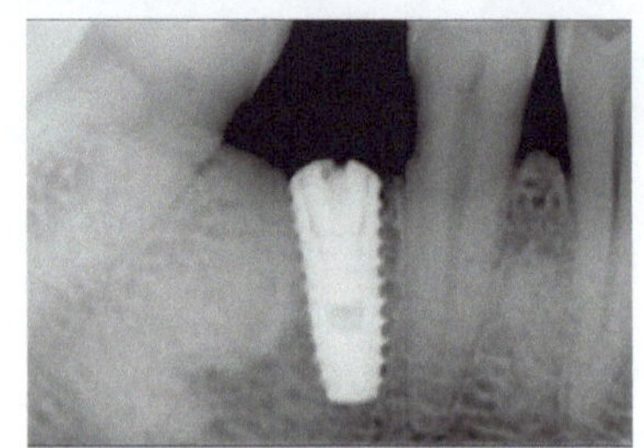 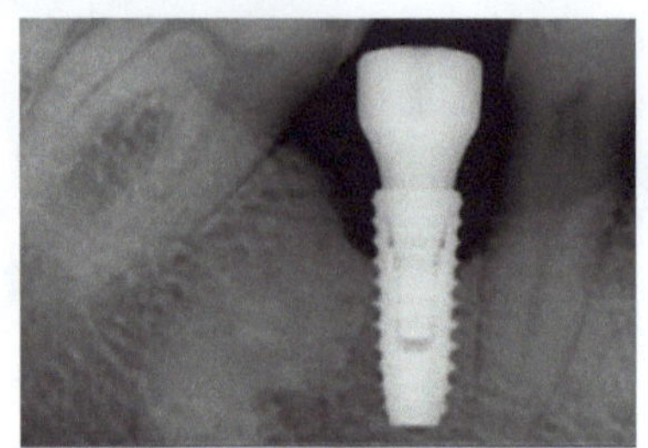

**PERI IMPLANTITIS - BONE LOSS
MOBILITY OF IMPLANT**

NEAR BY VITAL STRUCTRE

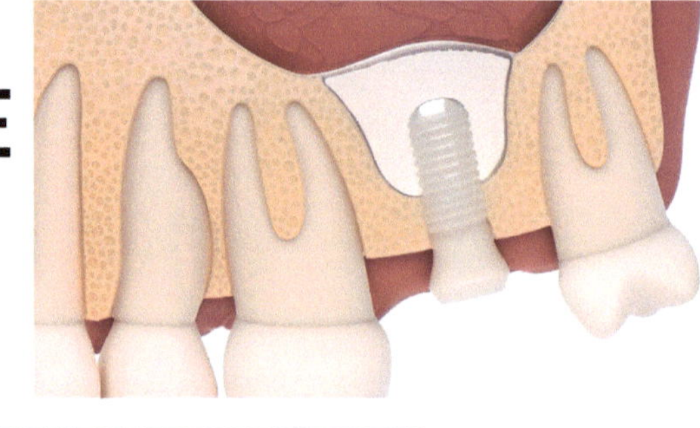

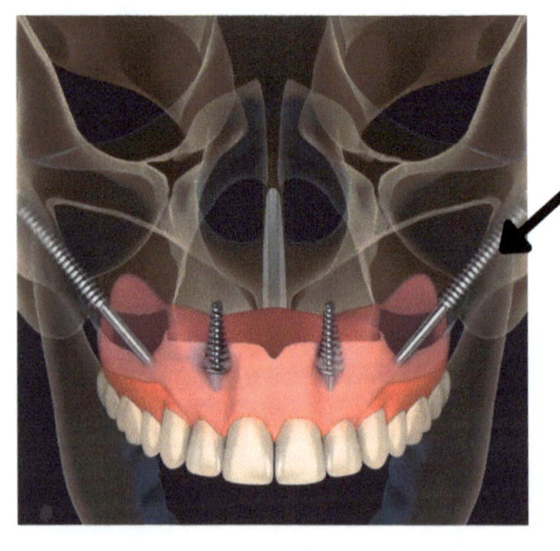

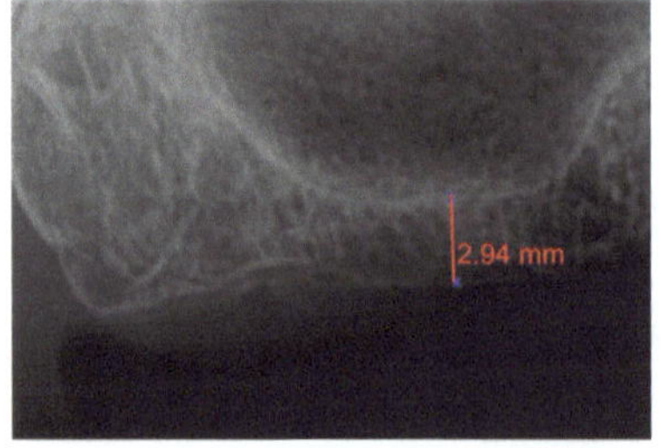

ZYGOMA IMPLANTS   INADEQUATE BONE

**BODY REJECTION
POOR ORAL HYGIENE
BONE DISEASE
INADEQUATE SPACE
UNCONTROLLED SYSTEMIC DISEASE**

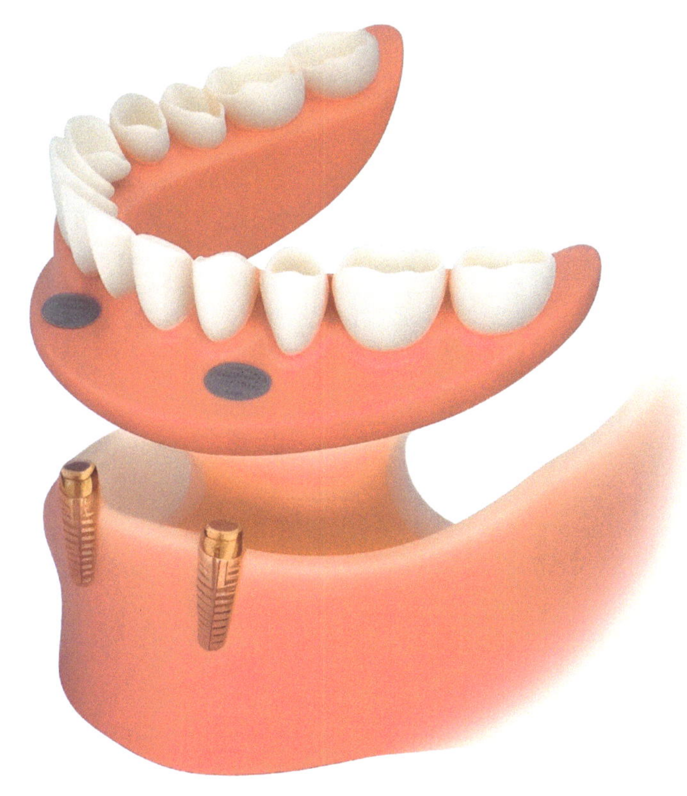

IMPLANT SUPPORTED DENTURE

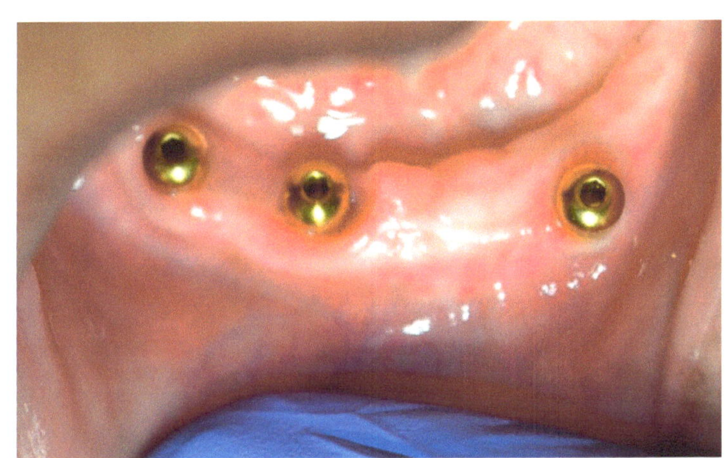

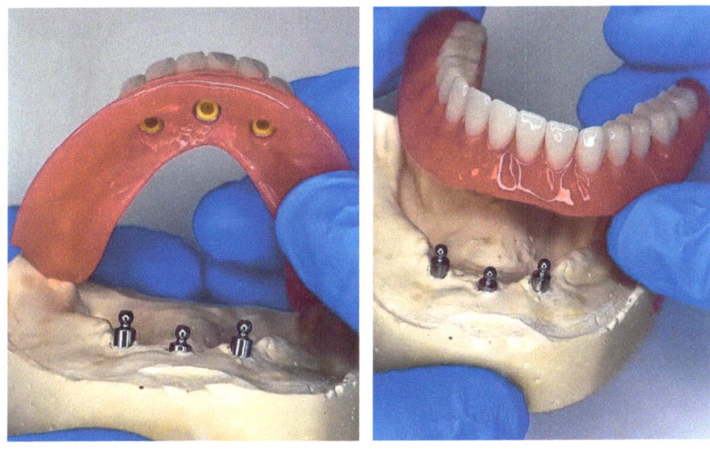

BALL ATTACHMENT

DENTAL POST & CORE

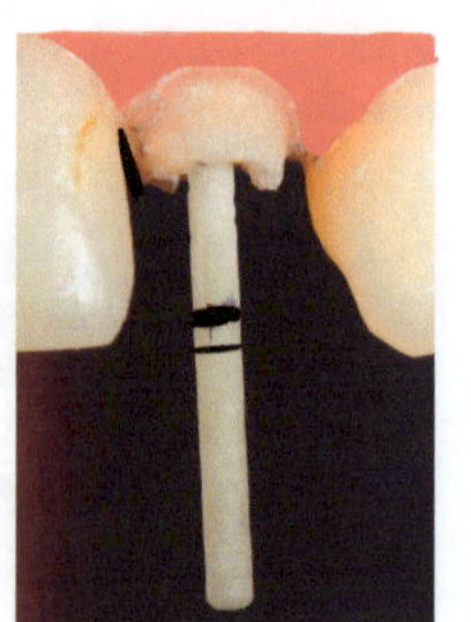

TO RESTORE TOOTH BACK TO FUNCTION

PIN LIKE RETENTIVE PART INSERTED IN TO TOOTH TO MAKE CROWN PORTION

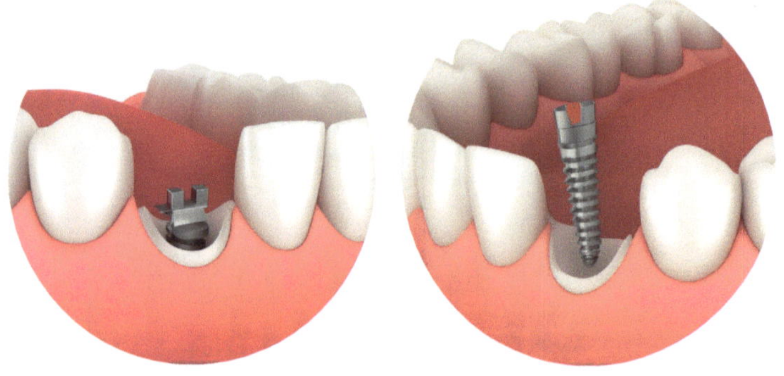

Retention and resistance Provider

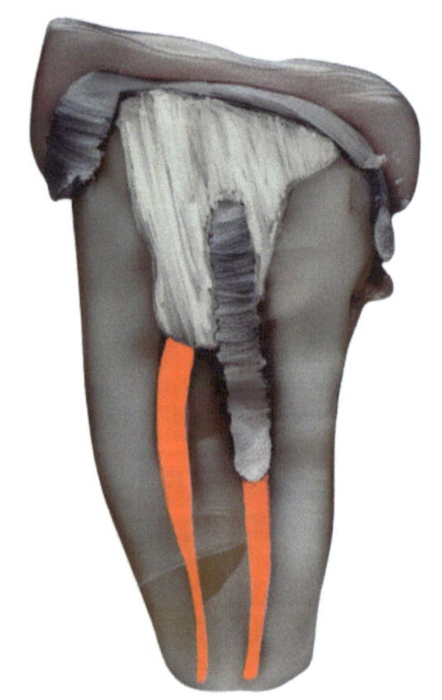

Specially where tooth structure is not enough

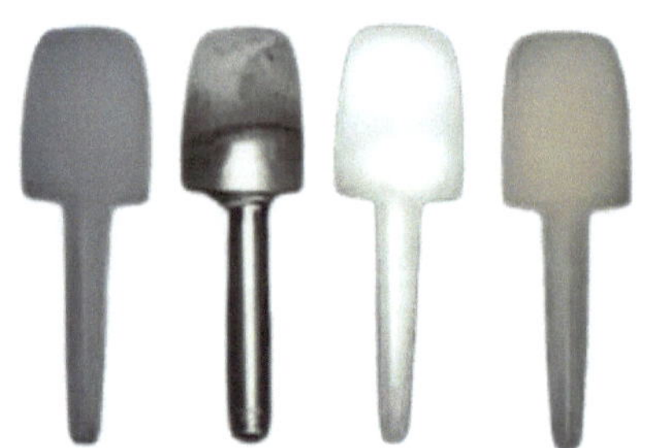

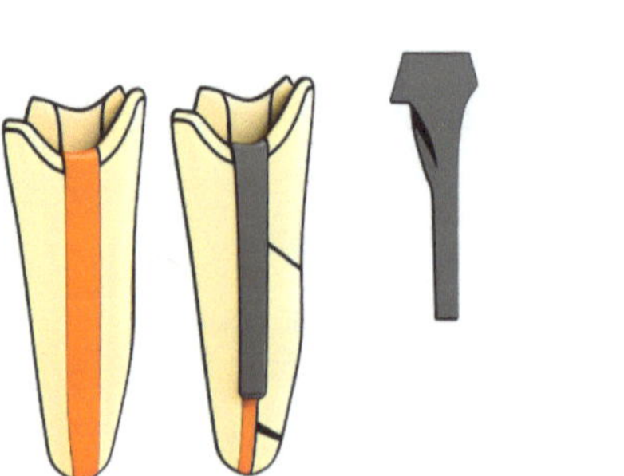

PERIODONTAL CARE | SCALING

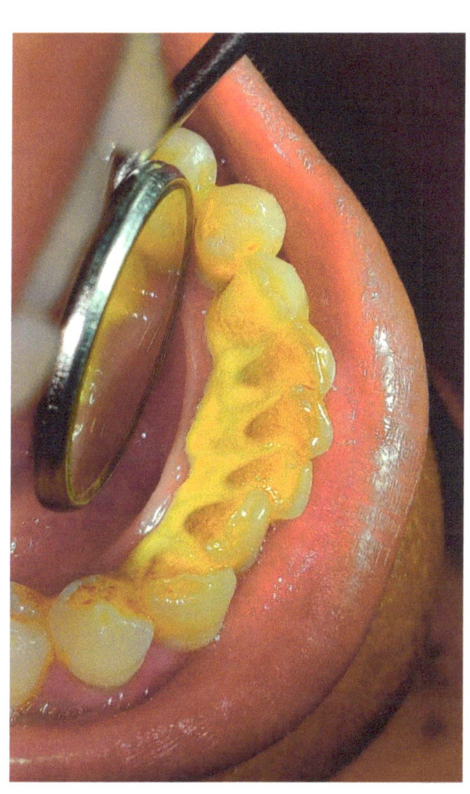

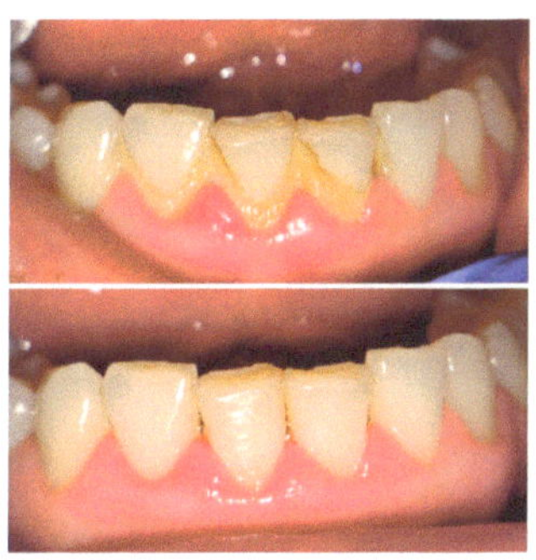

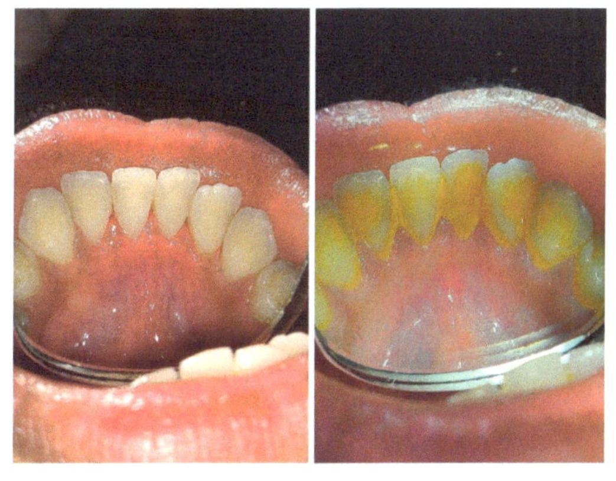

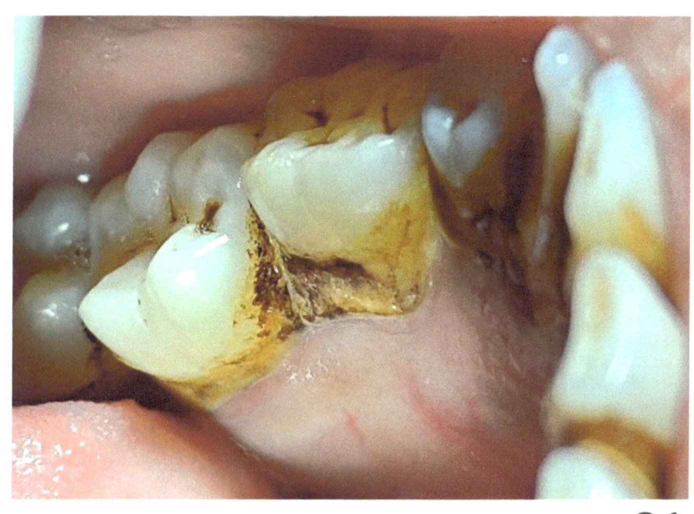

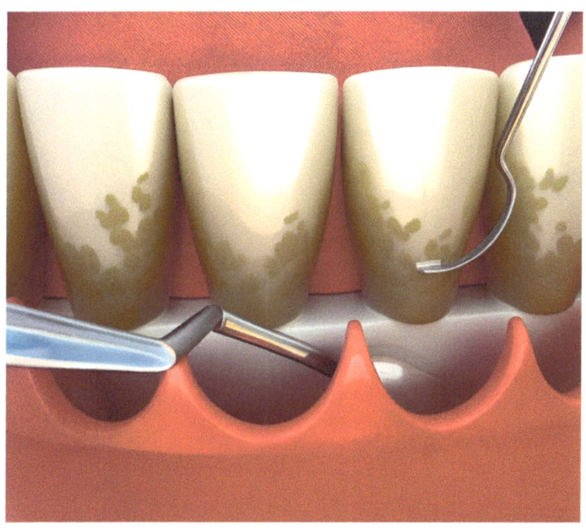

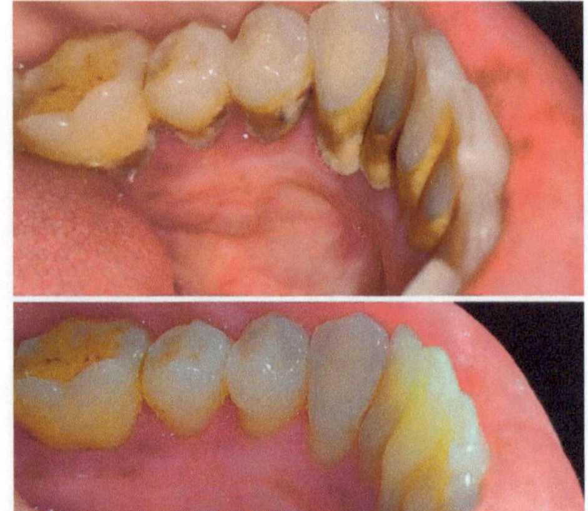
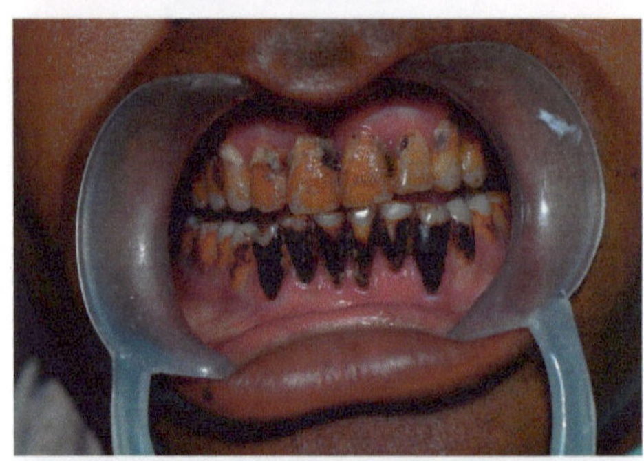

SCALING | CLEANING
Removal of extrinsic stains
Removal of debries, Calculus

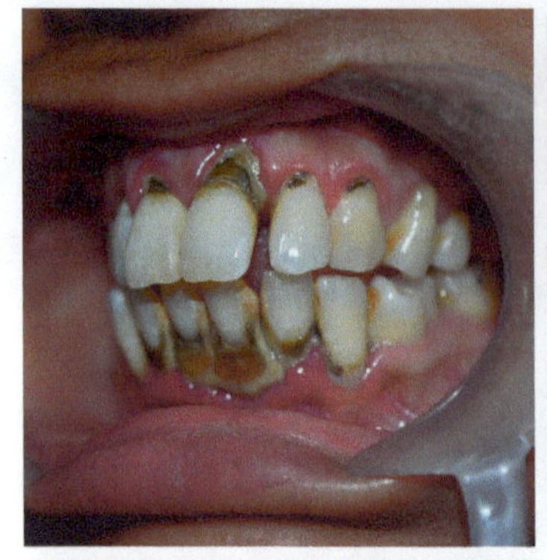
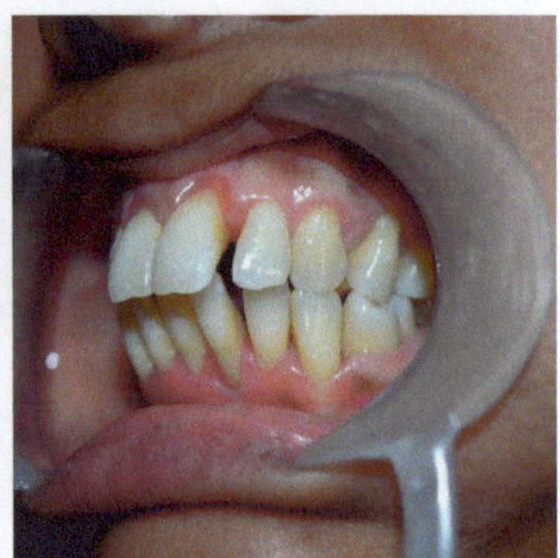

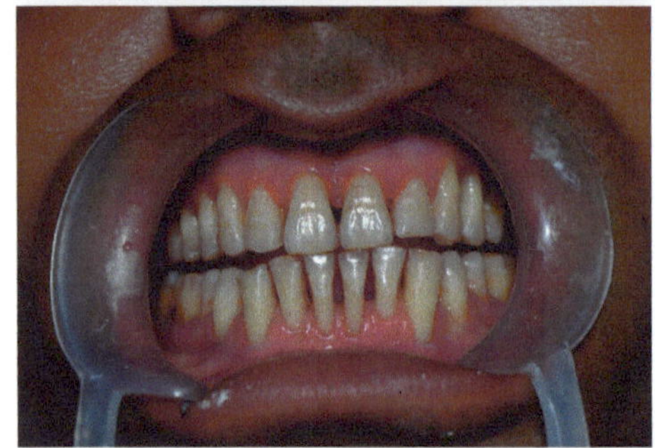

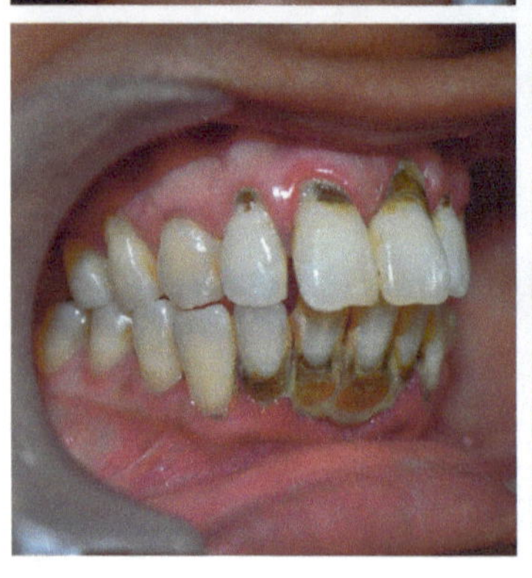
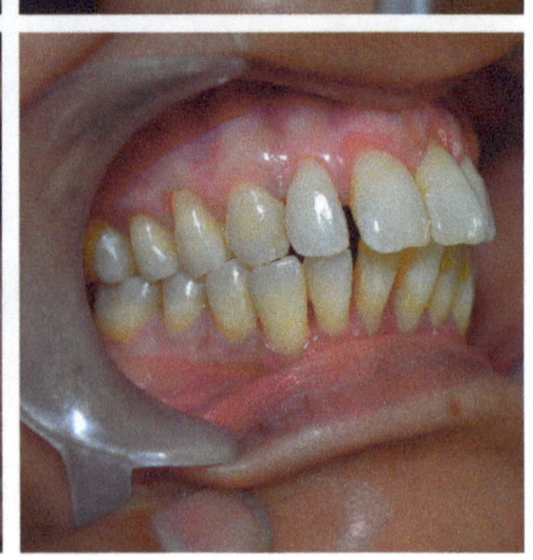

THIS KIND OF CONDITION REQUIRES MULTIPLE TIME FOLLOW-UP TO IMPROVE THE CONDITIONS.
THIS CONDITION MAY CAUSE GENERAL HEALTH PROBLEMS AND GENERAL HEALTH MAY ALSO CAUSE THIS CONDITION

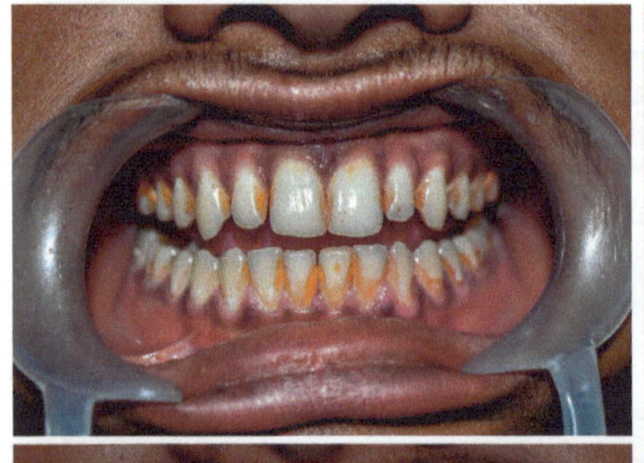
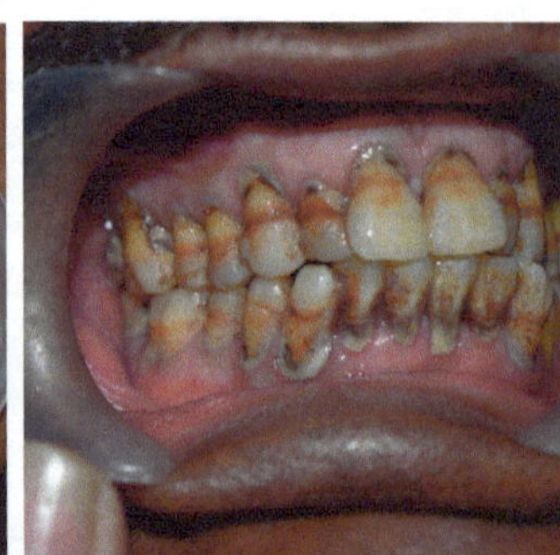
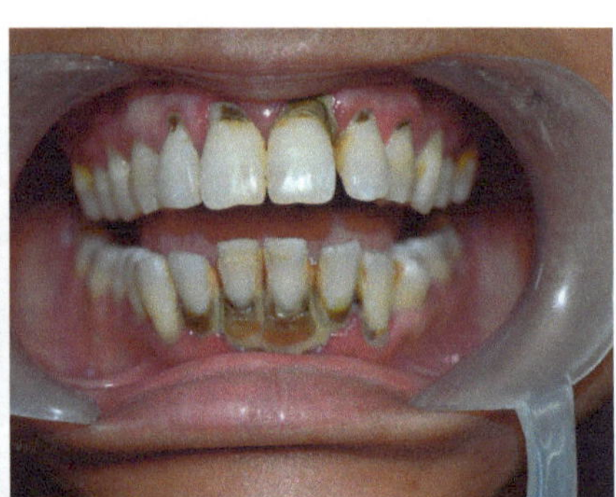

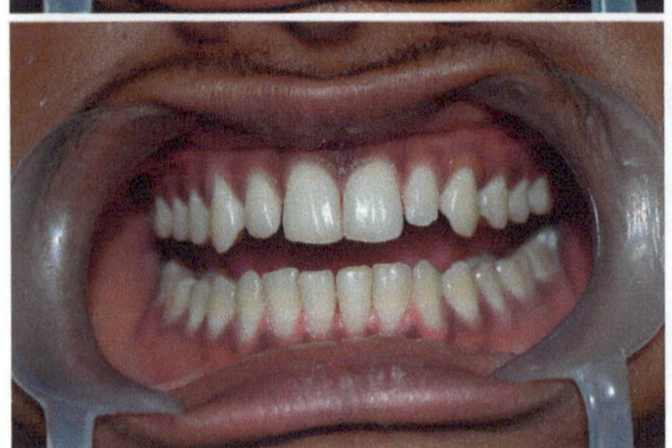
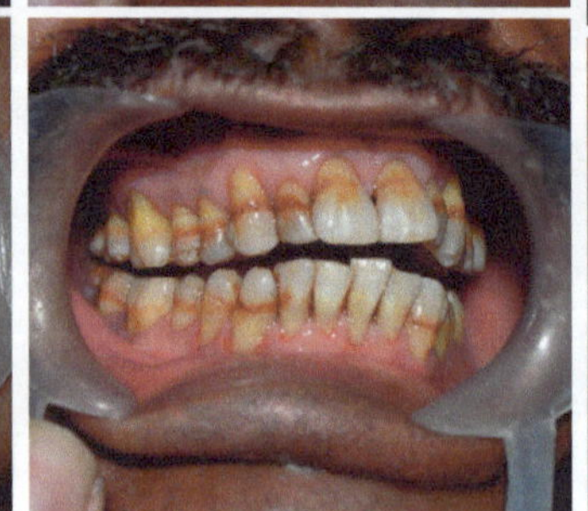
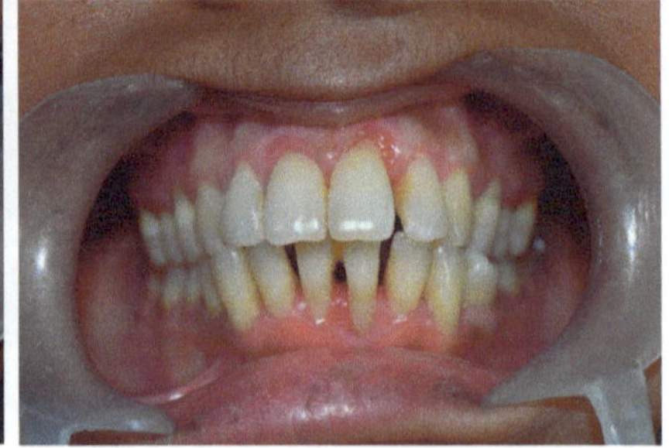

SENSITIVITY

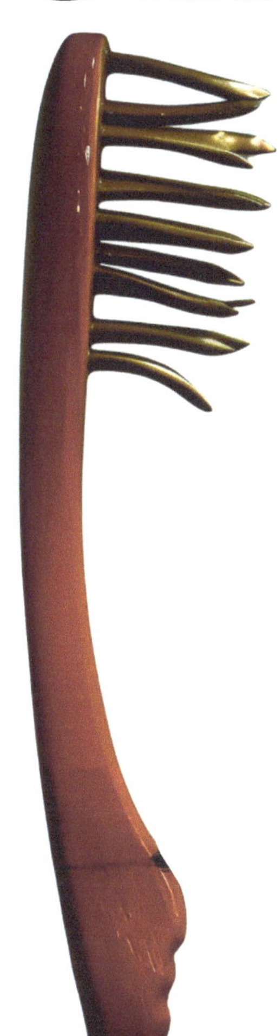

HARD BRUSHING
DOESN'T CLEAN BETTER

HARD BRISTLES ARE HARMFUL

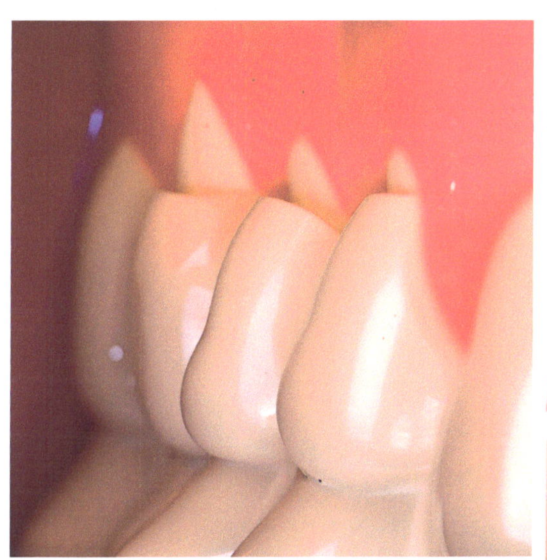

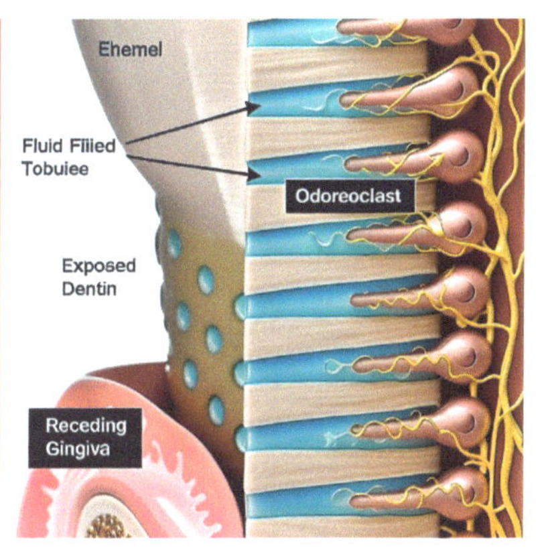

CAN CAUSE SENSITIVITY
MINOR SENSITIVITY CAN BE
CONTROLLED BY ANTI
SENSITIVITY PASTE AT SOME
LEVEL OR IT MAY REQUIRE
FILLING/RCT

CHANGE THE BRUSHING TECHANIQUE

INTERDENTAL BONE LOSS

FLAP SURGERY | CURETTAGE | BONE GRAFTING

1. What is Curettage? Curettage is a surgical procedure where a doctor uses a specialized instrument called a curette to scrape away abnormal tissue. This is often done to treat certain skin conditions, such as basal cell carcinoma, or to remove abnormal growths or infections. In some cases, it is used to clean out infected areas or remove debris.

- Why is curettage done?
- It is performed to remove abnormal or diseased tissue and promote healing of the area. This can be part of the treatment for skin cancers or for chronic infections or inflammatory conditions.
- How is curettage performed?
- The area is numbed with local anesthesia. Then, the curette (a spoon-shaped instrument) is used to carefully scrape away the abnormal tissue. After the procedure, a dressing may be applied to protect the area.
- Post-Procedure Care for Curettage:
  - Keep the area clean and dry.
  - Follow your doctor's instructions for wound care, such as applying prescribed ointments or creams.
  - Avoid scratching or picking at the area to prevent infection.
  - Monitor for signs of infection, such as increased redness, swelling, or pus.

2. What is Flap Surgery? Flap surgery is a procedure in which healthy tissue is moved from one part of the body to another to cover a wound or defect. This type of surgery is often used after a tumor has been removed, especially in areas like the skin or oral cavity, to help restore the function and appearance of the affected area.

- **Why is flap surgery done?**
- **Flap surgery** is used to close large wounds or defects, particularly when there is not enough healthy tissue around the wound to close it directly. It helps ensure better healing, reduces the risk of infection, and may improve the cosmetic outcome of the surgery.
- **How is flap surgery performed?**
    a. The surgeon will select a piece of healthy tissue from nearby areas, such as skin, muscle, or fat.
    b. This tissue is carefully lifted or "flapped" over the wound or defect to cover it.
    c. Blood vessels in the flap are carefully connected to maintain the tissue's blood supply.
    d. The flap is sutured in place to allow for proper healing.
- **Types of Flap Surgery:**
    e. Local flap: Tissue is moved from nearby to cover the wound.
    f. Regional flap: Tissue is taken from a more distant but still connected part of the body.
    g. Free flap: Tissue is completely detached and moved from one area to another, typically using a microvascular technique to reconnect blood vessels.
- **Post-Procedure Care for Flap Surgery:**
    h. Elevate the area as instructed to reduce swelling.
    i. Keep the wound clean and dry; follow the wound care instructions provided.
    j. Watch for signs of infection or flap failure, including unusual redness, increasing pain, or a change in the color of the flap tissue.
    k. Avoid placing pressure on the flap area during recovery.
    l. Follow-up visits are essential to ensure proper healing and flap viability.

Potential Risks and Complications: Both curettage and flap surgery are generally safe, but as with any surgical procedure, there are risks:

- **Infection**
- **Scarring or poor wound healing**
- **Bleeding**
- **Loss of the flap or graft (in flap surgery)**
- **Changes in sensation or function (depending on the location of surgery)**

4. Recovery and Outlook:

- **Curettage: Most people recover quickly, and the wound heals over a few weeks. The area may remain red for some time but should gradually return to normal.**
- **Flap Surgery: Recovery from flap surgery can take longer, with full healing often taking several weeks to months, depending on the size of the flap and the complexity of the surgery. Some swelling and discomfort are common during the early stages of recovery.**

BONE GRAFTING

Bone grafting is a surgical procedure used to restore or rebuild bone tissue that has been lost due to injury, disease, or a lack of sufficient bone volume for dental implants. This is commonly performed in areas around the teeth (interdental) or where dental implants are being placed.

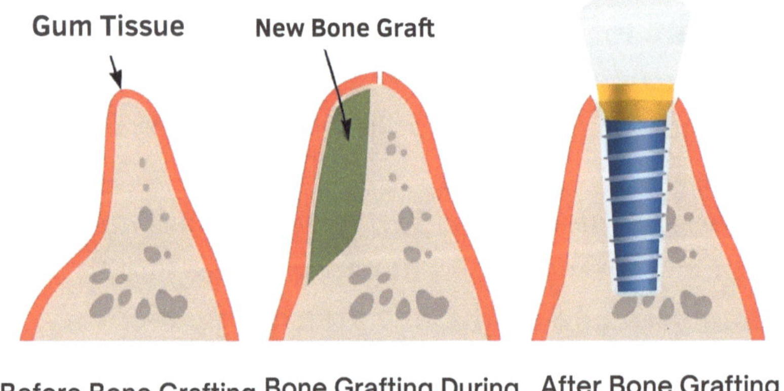

Before Bone Grafting   Bone Grafting During the Healing Process   After Bone Grafting with Implant

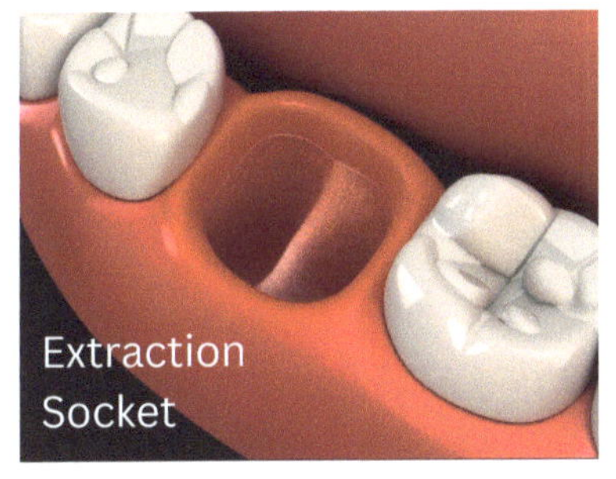

BONE GRAFTING

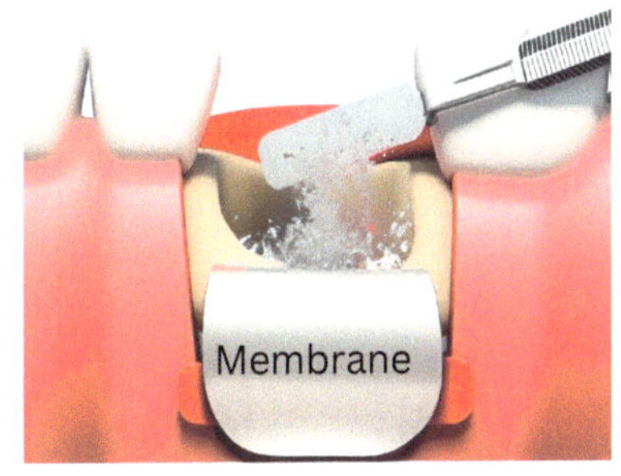

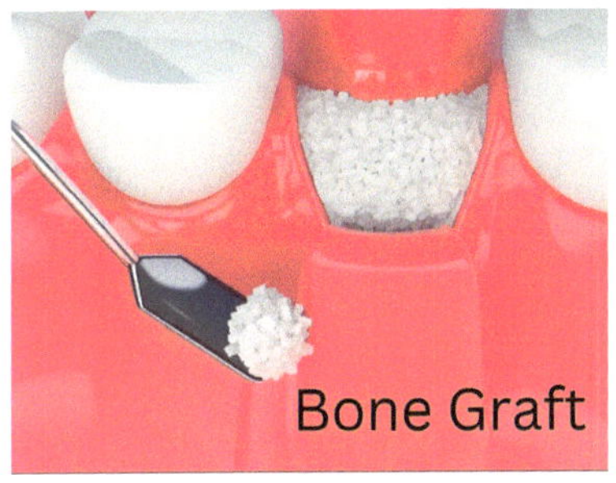

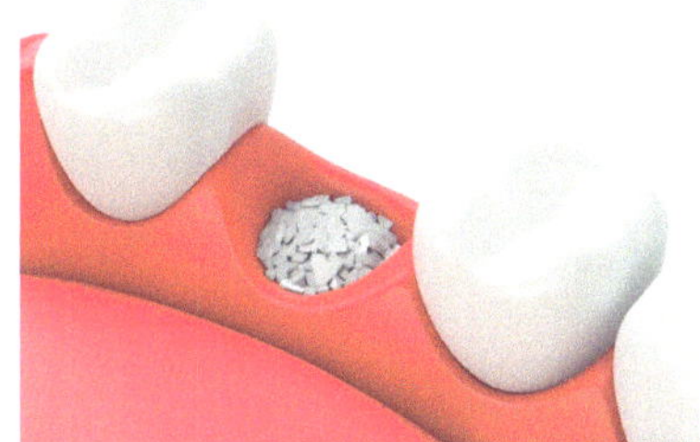

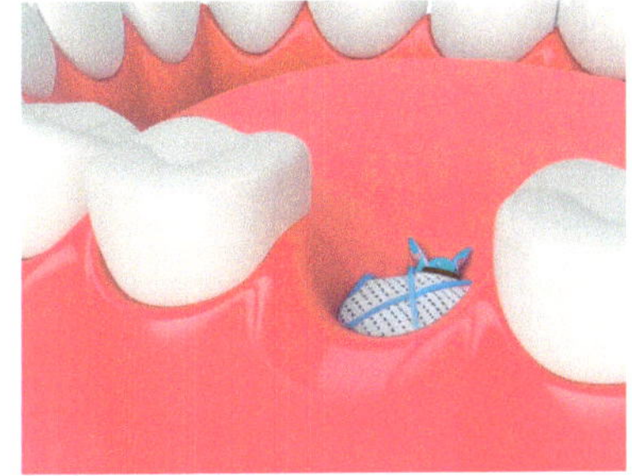

SOCKET
PRESERVATION

Visible bone loss and loss of stability

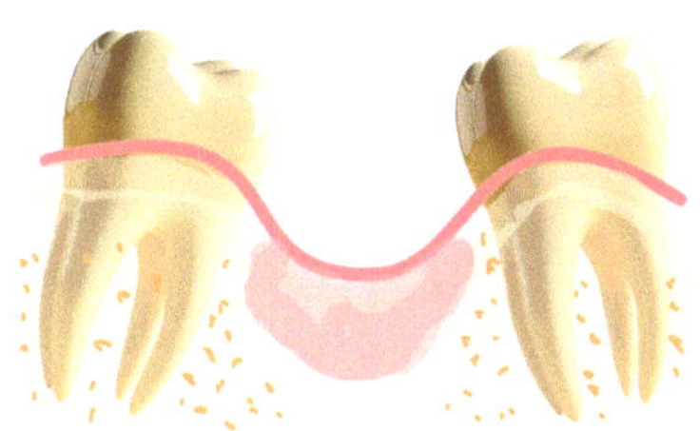

After bone grafting

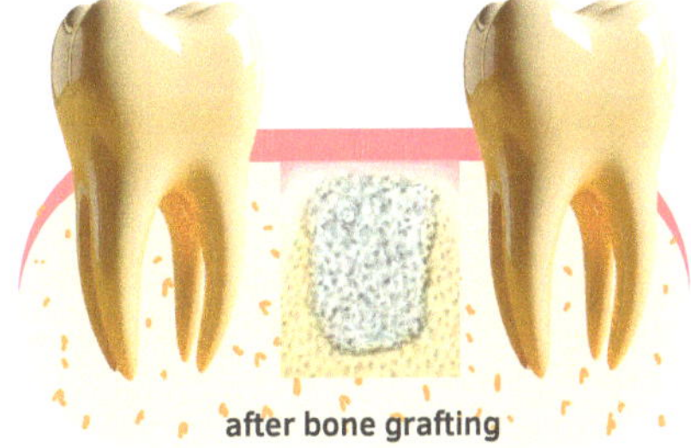

Can Support teeth and surrounding tissue

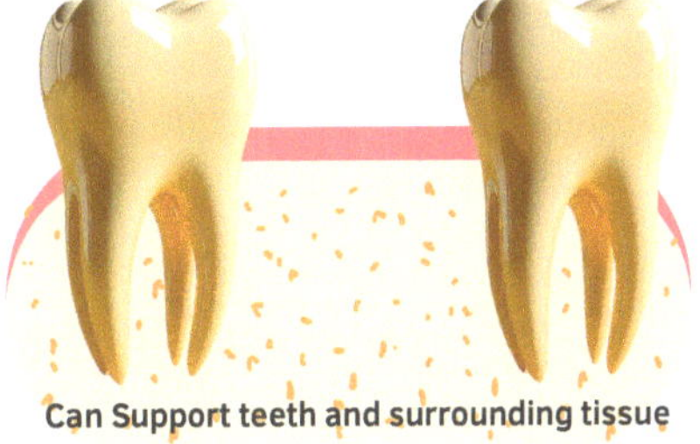

EXTRACTION

PATIENT MUST BE PHYSICALLY FIT FOR TOOTH REMOVAL

PATIENT MUST HAVE TAKEN ENOUGH MEAL BEFORE TOOTH REMOVAL UNDER LOCAL ANAESTHESIA

CARE SHOULD BE TAKEN BEFORE AND AFTER EXTRACTION AS PER DOCTOR S INSTRUCTIONS

PATIENT MUST INFORM ABOUT **MEDICAL AND DENTAL HISTORY** SO DOCTOR CAN PROVIDE BETTER TREATMENT

PLEASE BRING ANY MEDICATIONS YOU ARE CURRENTLY TAKING FOR ANY MEDICAL CONDITION.

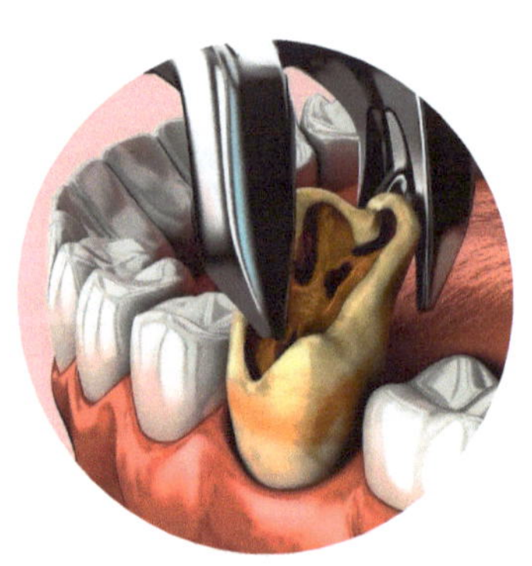

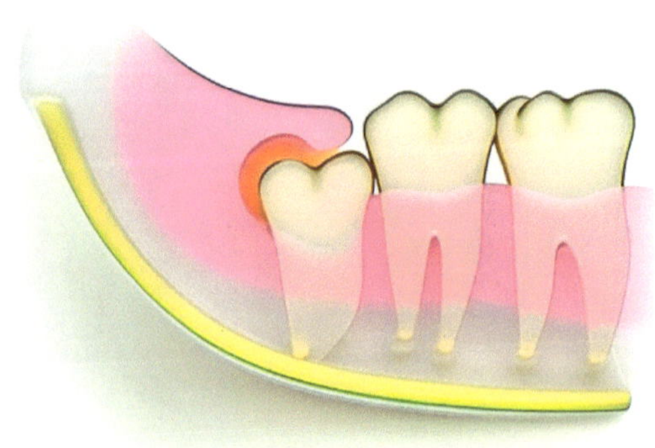

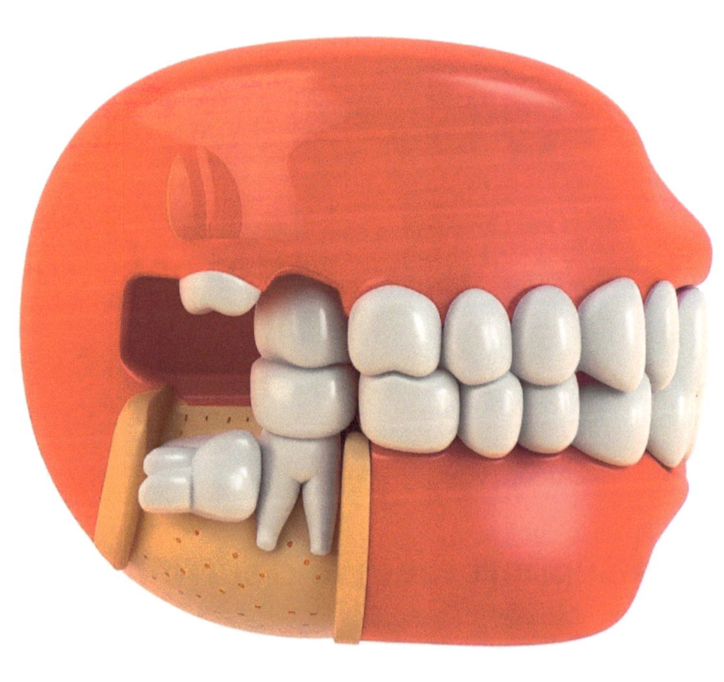

POST-TOOTH REMOVAL CARE INSTRUCTIONS:
1. **BITE ON GAUZE:**
   - KEEP THE GAUZE PAD PLACED OVER THE EXTRACTION SITE FOR 30-45 MINUTES. THIS HELPS CONTROL BLEEDING AND AIDS IN CLOT FORMATION. IF BLEEDING CONTINUES, REPLACE THE GAUZE AND BITE DOWN FIRMLY FOR ANOTHER 30 MINUTES.
2. **AVOID RINSING OR SPITTING:**
   - DO NOT RINSE YOUR MOUTH, SPIT, OR USE MOUTHWASH FOR THE FIRST 24 HOURS, AS THIS CAN DISTURB THE CLOT AND LEAD TO DRY SOCKET.
3. **APPLY ICE:**
   - TO MINIMIZE SWELLING, APPLY AN ICE PACK ON THE OUTSIDE OF YOUR FACE NEAR THE EXTRACTION AREA FOR 10 MINUTES, THEN REMOVE IT FOR 10 MINUTES. REPEAT AS NEEDED FOR THE FIRST 24 HOURS.
4. **TAKE PRESCRIBED MEDICATIONS:**
   - TAKE PAIN RELIEVERS OR ANTIBIOTICS AS PRESCRIBED BY YOUR DENTIST TO MANAGE PAIN AND PREVENT INFECTION.
5. **EAT SOFT FOODS:**
   - WAIT FOR ANAESTHESIA EFFECT COME BACK TO NORMAL.STICK TO SOFT FOODS LIKE YOGURT, SOUPS, AND MASHED POTATOES FOR THE FIRST FEW DAYS. AVOID HOT, SPICY, AND CRUNCHY FOODS. GRADUALLY REINTRODUCE SOLID FOODS AS THE EXTRACTION SITE HEALS.
6. **AVOID SMOKING AND ALCOHOL:**
   - DO NOT SMOKE OR DRINK ALCOHOL FOR AT LEAST 48 HOURS, AS THEY CAN DELAY HEALING AND INCREASE THE RISK OF COMPLICATIONS LIKE DRY SOCKET.
7. **DO NOT USE STRAWS:**
   - AVOID USING STRAWS FOR 48 HOURS TO PREVENT DISLODGING THE BLOOD CLOT.
8. **ELEVATE YOUR HEAD:**
   - KEEP YOUR HEAD ELEVATED WITH PILLOWS WHEN LYING DOWN TO MINIMIZE SWELLING.
9. **RINSE WITH SALT WATER:**
   - AFTER 24 HOURS, RINSE YOUR MOUTH GENTLY WITH WARM SALT WATER (1 TEASPOON OF SALT IN A GLASS OF WATER) SEVERAL TIMES A DAY, ESPECIALLY AFTER MEALS, TO KEEP THE AREA CLEAN.
10. **MONITOR FOR COMPLICATIONS:**
   - CONTACT YOUR DENTIST IF YOU EXPERIENCE EXCESSIVE BLEEDING, SEVERE PAIN, FEVER, OR SWELLING THAT WORSENS AFTER 2-3 DAYS.

WISDOM TOOTH

THIRD MOLAR

WISDOM TEETH, OR THIRD MOLARS, OFTEN LACK SPACE TO ERUPT PROPERLY, CAUSING PAIN, SWELLING, OR INFECTION. EXTRACTION IS A MINOR SURGICAL PROCEDURE PERFORMED UNDER LOCAL ANESTHESIA TO ENSURE COMFORT DURING THE PROCESS. AFTER THE PROCEDURE, PROPER CARE, SUCH AS AVOIDING SMOKING AND FOLLOWING A SOFT DIET, ENSURES SMOOTH HEALING. CONTACT YOUR DENTIST IF YOU NOTICE EXCESSIVE BLEEDING, SWELLING, OR SEVERE PAIN.

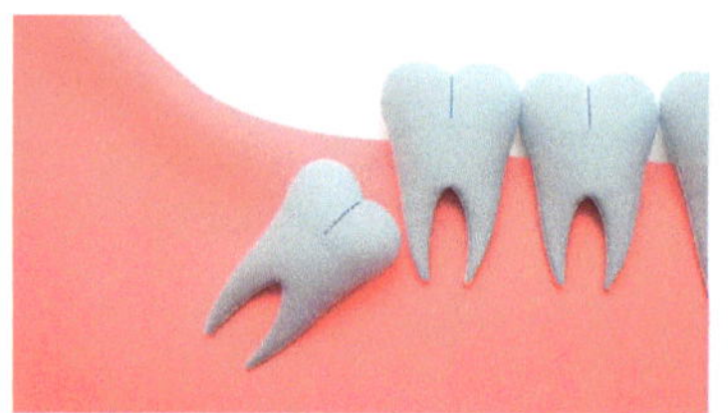
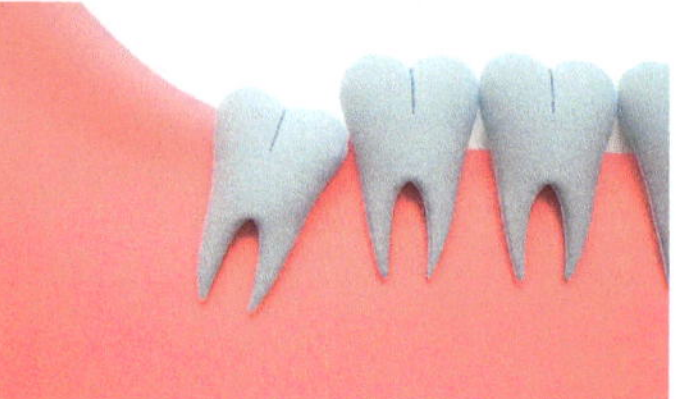
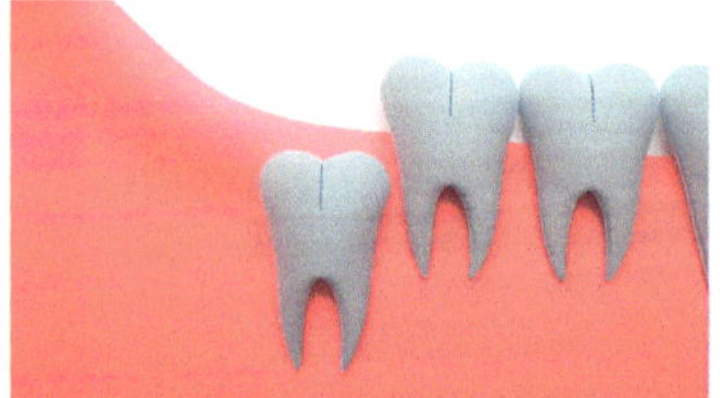
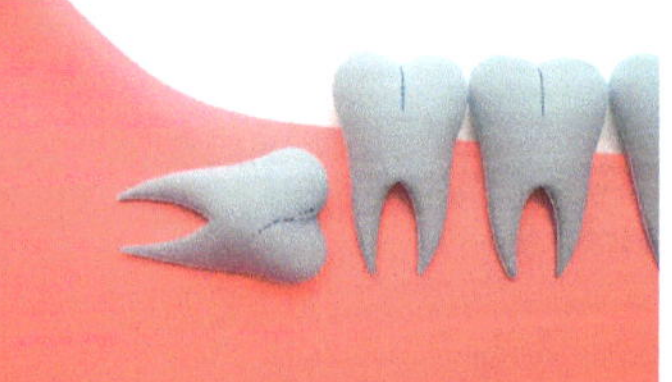

PERICORONITIS

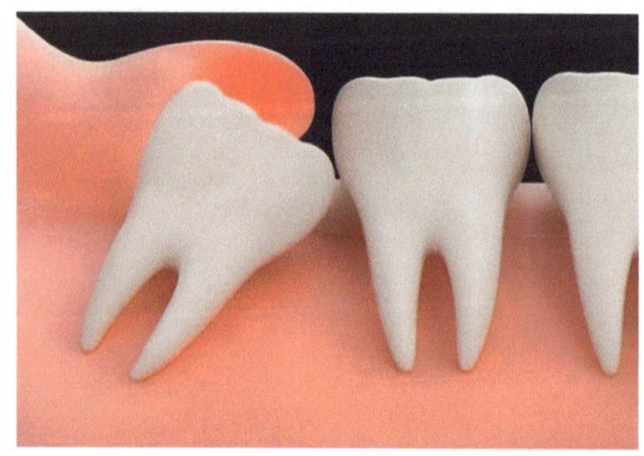

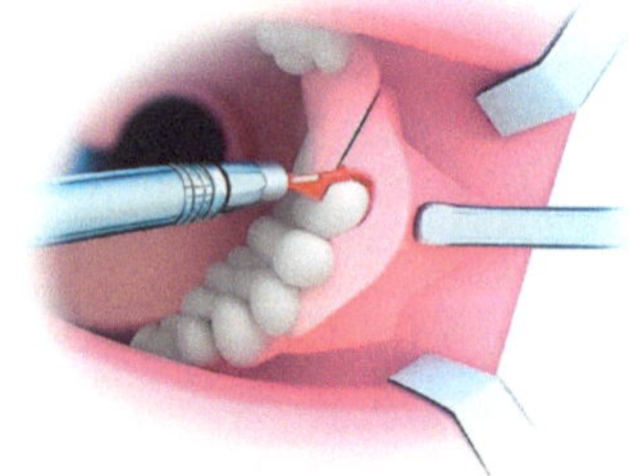
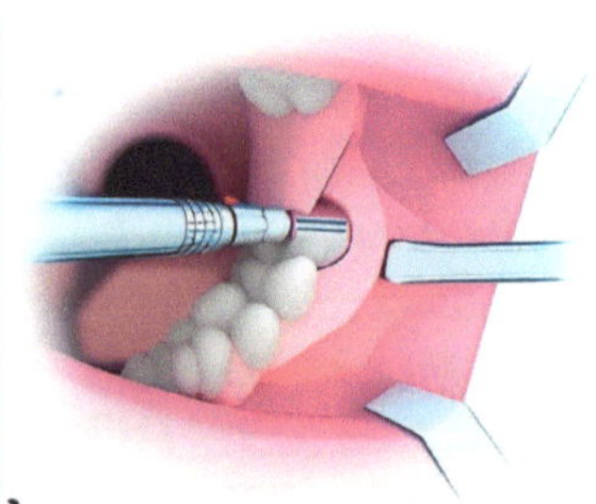
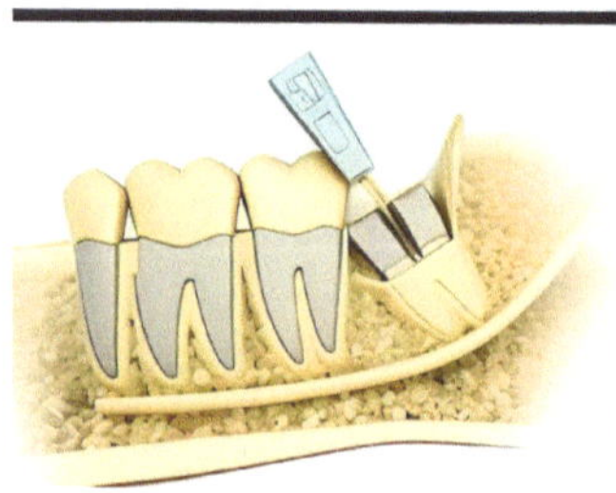
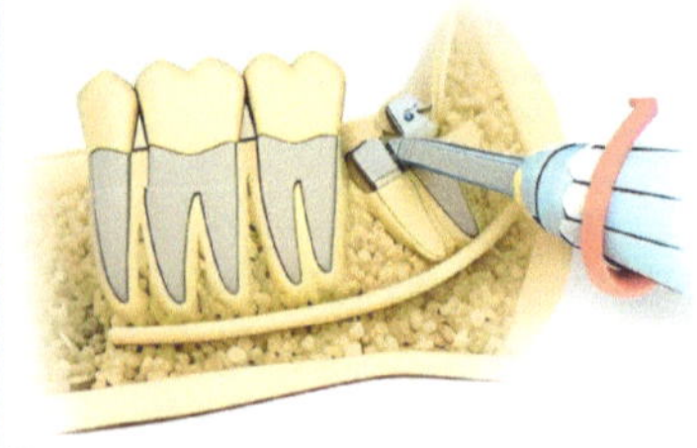

WHY STRAIGHT TEETH ARE REQUIRED?

DAILY SELF CLEANSING IS MORE IMPORTANT

TEETH ALIGNMENT HELPS IN MAINTAINANCE OF ORAL HYGIENE

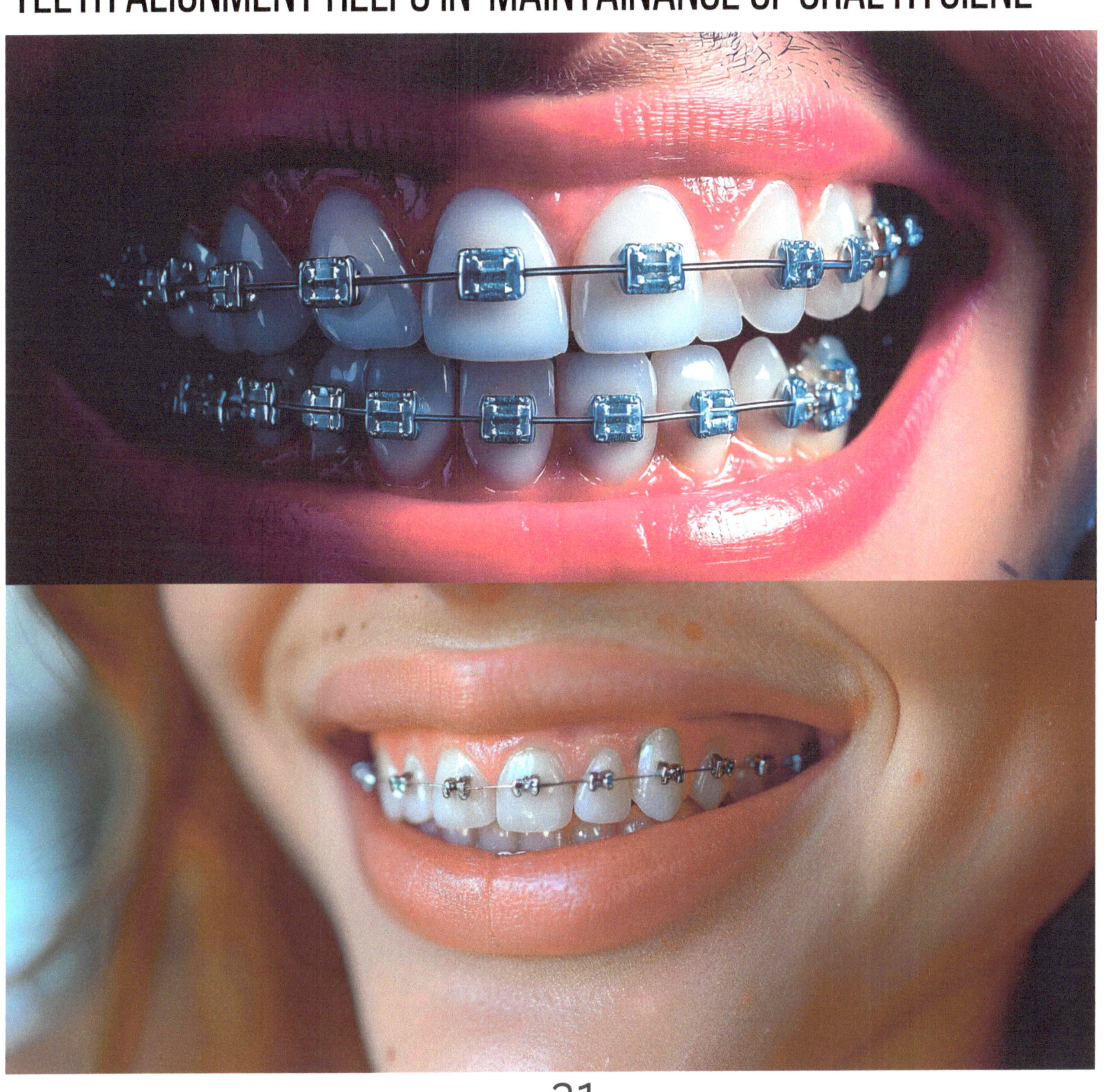

Straight teeth are important for a number of reasons, including:

Reduced risk of injury
Straight teeth are less likely to be broken or fractured in accidents, falls, and sports.

Easier to clean
Straight teeth are easier to brush and floss, which reduces the risk of tooth decay and gum disease.

Improved bite
Straight teeth chew properly, which can reduce the risk of biting your tongue or knocking out a tooth.

Reduced risk of jaw problems
Crooked teeth can strain the jaw joints, leading to pain, headaches, dizziness, and earaches.

Healthier gums
Crooked teeth can put pressure on the gum line, making them more difficult to clean and increasing the risk of gum disease.

Improved airway
Orthodontic treatment can help with sleep apnea caused by jaw or craniofacial abnormalities.

Stronger jawbone
Straightening teeth can help prevent the breakdown of the jawbone bones that support the teeth.

Space for dental implants
Orthodontic treatment can create space for dental implants, which can restore the ability to chew and speak.

If you have crooked or crowded teeth, you should talk to your dentist about the best teeth straightening option for you.

ORTHODONTICS

TEETH ALIGNMENT HELPS IN MAINTAINANCE OF ORAL HYGIENE

BRACES AND ALIGNERS
REMOVABLE APPLIANCES
FIXED APPLIANCES
EXTRA ORAL APPLIANCES

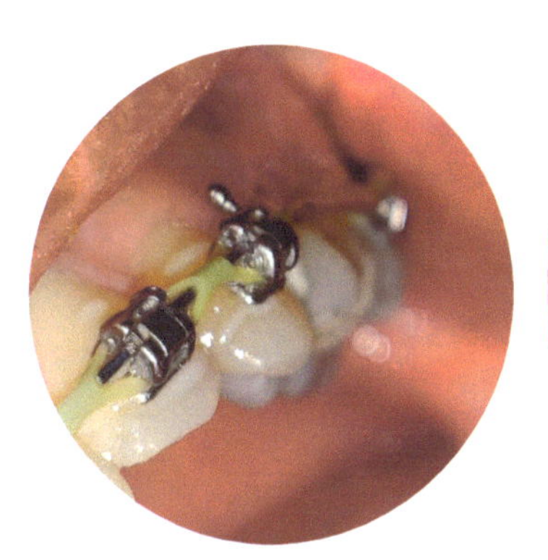
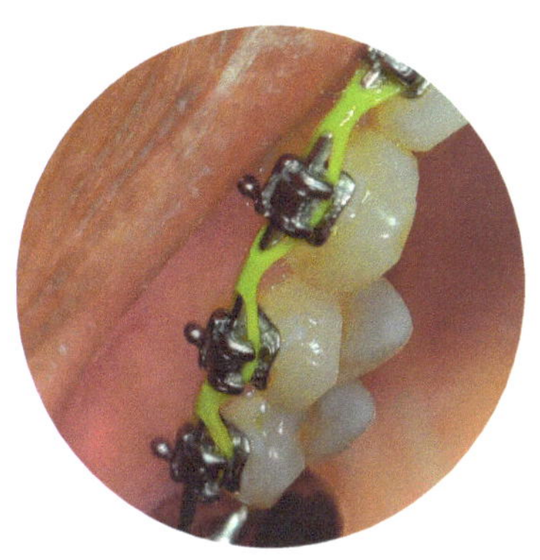

WIRES AND BRACKETS ARE USED TO MOVE THE NATURAL TEETH IN PERTICULAR POSITION, FIXED TYPE REQUIRES REGULAR PRISCRIBED INTERVAL

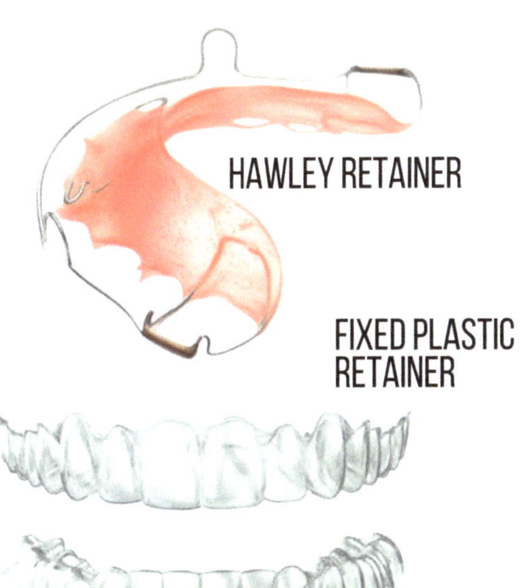

HAWLEY RETAINER

FIXED PLASTIC RETAINER

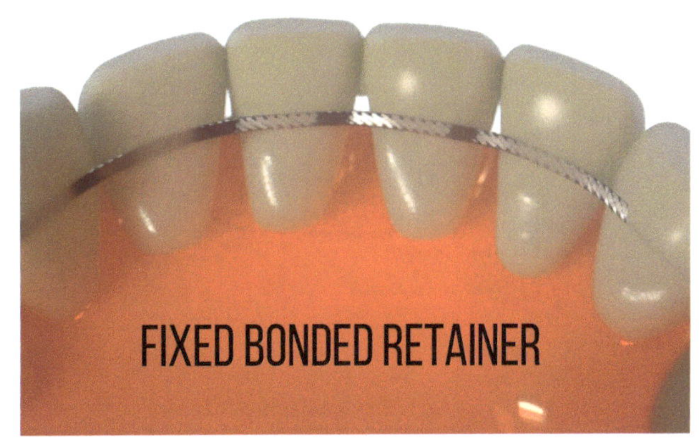

METAL BRACES

CERAMIC BRACES

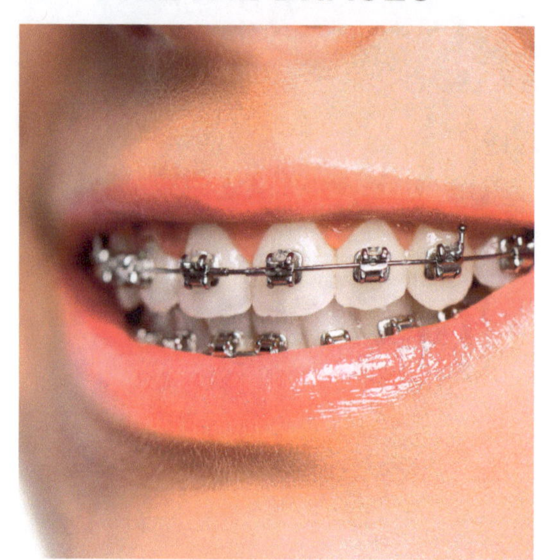

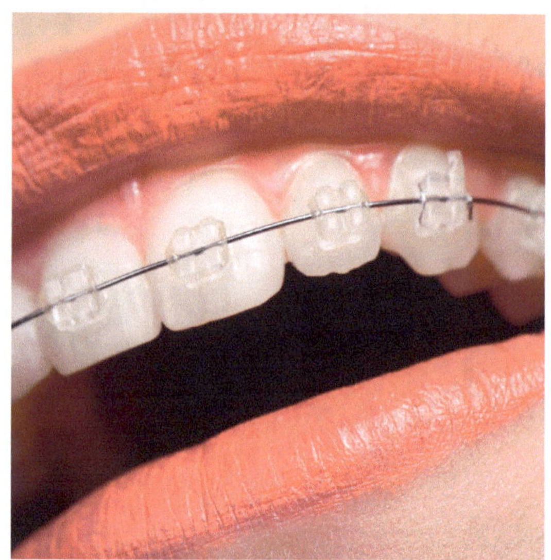

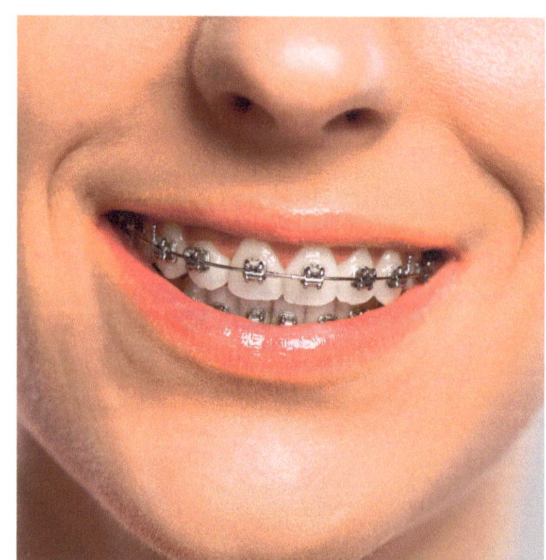

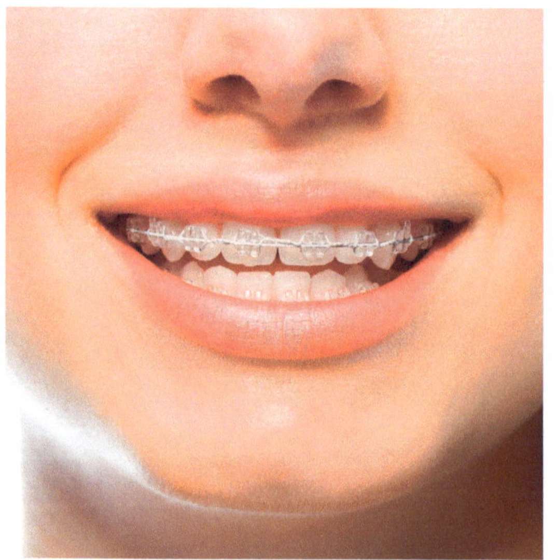

RETAINERS

Retainers play a crucial role in maintaining the results after orthodontic treatment, such as braces or aligners. Here's key information and the importance of retainers for patient education:

What are Retainers?
Retainers are custom-made dental appliances designed to hold your teeth in their new positions after orthodontic treatment. They can be either removable or fixed (permanent) and are typically worn after teeth have been straightened with braces or aligners.

Importance of Wearing Retainers
1. Prevent Teeth from Shifting: After braces or aligners are removed, teeth tend to move back to their original positions. Retainers help prevent this by maintaining the alignment achieved during treatment.
2. Stabilizing Teeth: Once teeth have been moved, the surrounding bone and tissue need time to stabilize. Wearing retainers helps teeth stay in place as the bones and tissues adapt to their new positions.
3. Maintaining Your Investment: Orthodontic treatment is a significant investment of time and money. Wearing a retainer ensures that the results of the treatment are maintained long-term, protecting your investment.
4. Prevent Relapse: Without retainers, there is a risk of relapse, where teeth shift back to their pre-treatment positions, requiring further corrective treatment.

Types of Retainers
1. *Removable Retainers*:
   - Hawley Retainers: Made of acrylic and a thin metal wire, they are durable and easy to adjust. The wire wraps around the teeth to hold them in place.
   - Clear Plastic Retainers (Essix): Similar to aligners, these are made of transparent plastic and are less noticeable. They are custom-fit to the shape of your teeth and are often used after clear aligner treatment.
2. *Fixed (Permanent) Retainers:*
   - These consist of a thin wire bonded to the back of the front teeth (typically on the lower teeth). They are not visible from the front and are ideal for patients who need long-term retention without the responsibility of removing a retainer daily.

Retainer Wear Guidelines
- Consistency is Key: In the first few months after orthodontic treatment, retainers are typically worn full-time (day and night), except while eating, brushing, or flossing.
- Long-Term Use: After the initial period, many orthodontists recommend wearing retainers at night indefinitely to prevent relapse, as teeth can naturally shift over time.
- Follow Your Orthodontist's Instructions: Wear and care schedules can vary depending on the patient, so it's important to follow the specific instructions provided by the orthodontist.

Caring for Retainers
- *Clean Regularly:* Removable retainers should be cleaned daily using a soft toothbrush and non-abrasive toothpaste or mild soap. Do not use hot water, as it may warp the plastic.
- *Store Properly:* Always store retainers in their case when not in use. Avoid wrapping them in tissue, as they can easily be lost or thrown away.
- *Regular Check-Ups:* Have your retainers checked periodically by your orthodontist to ensure they are still fitting well and functioning properly.

FAQs for Patients
1. *How long do I need to wear retainers?*
   - You'll likely need to wear retainers for the rest of your life, but after the first year, most patients only need to wear them at night.
2. *Can I eat with a retainer in?*
   - Removable retainers should be taken out while eating to avoid damage. Permanent retainers, however, stay in place, but you should avoid hard, sticky foods.
3. *What happens if I lose or damage my retainer?*
   - Contact your orthodontist immediately. Wearing a damaged or ill-fitting retainer can be ineffective, and going without a retainer for too long may cause teeth to shift.

Conclusion
Retainers are essential for maintaining the results of your orthodontic treatment. Regular use and proper care of retainers will help ensure that your teeth stay aligned and that you continue to enjoy the benefits of a straight smile for years to come.

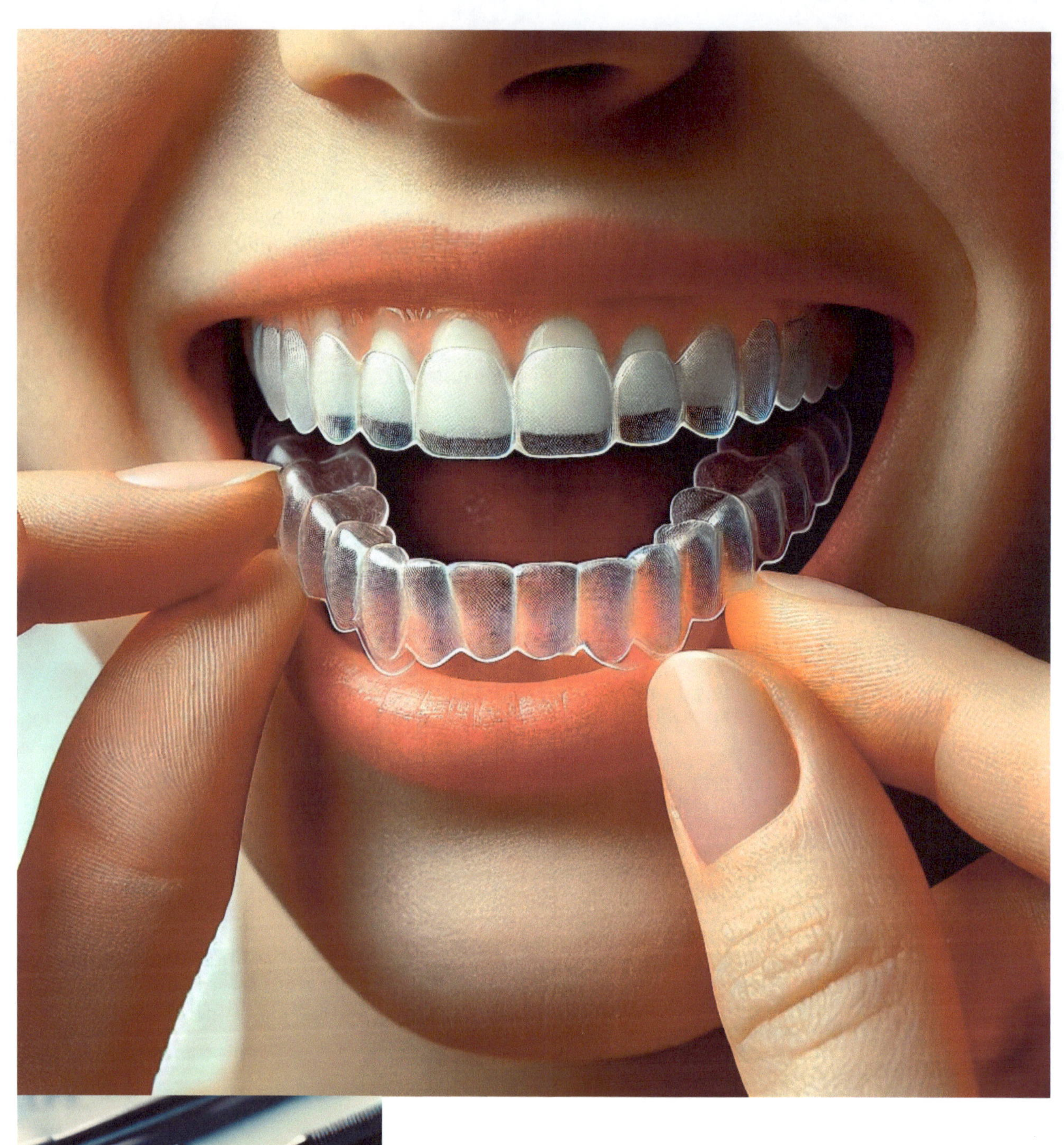

ALIGNERS

ALIGNERS

Dental aligners are a modern and convenient option for straightening teeth without the need for traditional metal braces.

What are Dental Aligners?

Dental aligners are clear, removable trays that fit snugly over your teeth and gradually shift them into proper alignment. They are custom-made for each patient using digital scans or impressions of the teeth.

How Do Aligners Work?

1. Custom-Fit Trays: Based on the patient's dental structure, a series of aligner trays are created, each designed to move teeth slightly.
2. Gradual Shifts: Each tray is worn for 1-2 weeks, applying gentle pressure to specific teeth, and then replaced by the next set.
3. Treatment Duration: The treatment typically lasts between 6-24 months, depending on the complexity of the case.

Benefits of Dental Aligners

- Aesthetic Appeal: They are nearly invisible, making them more cosmetically appealing than traditional braces.
- Removability: Aligners can be removed while eating, brushing, or flossing, which makes dental hygiene easier.
- Comfort: Made from smooth plastic, they are more comfortable than metal braces, which may cause irritation.
- Fewer Office Visits: Aligners often require fewer dental appointments compared to braces adjustments.

Instructions for Patients

- Wear Time: Aligners should be worn for 20-22 hours per day for effective results.
- Cleaning: Rinse aligners with lukewarm water and use a soft brush to clean them daily. Avoid hot water, as it can warp the plastic.
- Oral Hygiene: Brush and floss teeth after every meal before reinserting aligners to prevent trapping food particles and bacteria.
- Check-Ups: Regular check-ups with the dentist or orthodontist are essential to monitor progress.

Limitations

- Not for Everyone: Severe dental issues, like large gaps or misalignments, might require traditional braces or surgery.
- Discipline: Aligners are removable, so it's essential to be disciplined about wearing them to ensure success.

Common FAQs

1. *Are aligners painful?*
   - You may experience mild discomfort as your teeth move, especially when switching to a new set, but it usually subsides after a few days.
2. *How long will treatment take?*
   - Treatment time varies, but most people wear aligners for 12-18 months, depending on their dental condition.
3. *Can I eat and drink with aligners?*
   - You should remove aligners while eating or drinking anything other than water to avoid staining or damaging them.

Aligners offer an effective, convenient, and less noticeable way to achieve a better smile.

TEETH WHITENING

CLEANING AND WHITENING OF TEETH BOTH ARE DIFFERENT THINGS

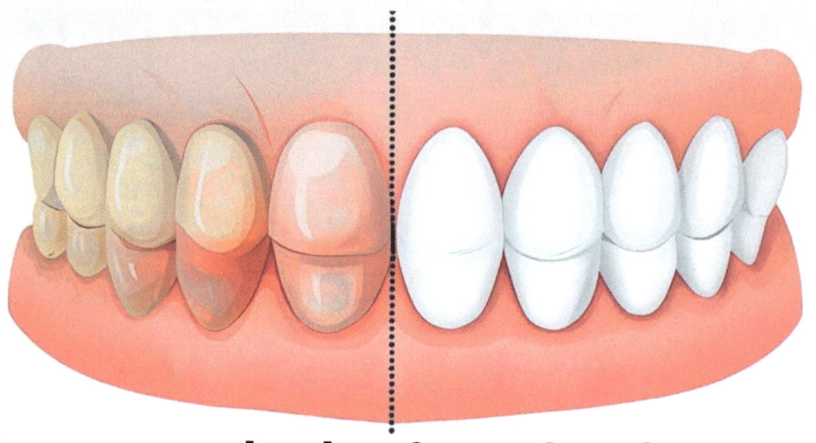

Different Methods of Teeth Whitening

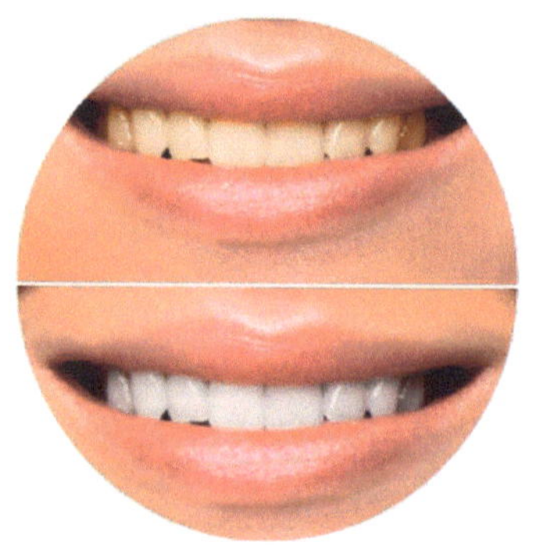

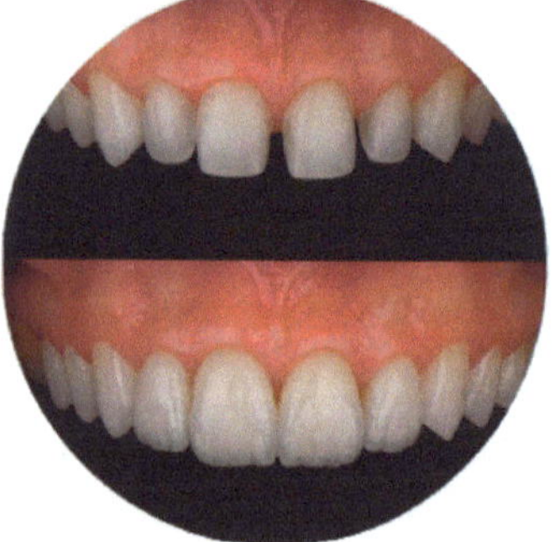

Bleaching

Home / Professional

Composite Veneers

in office

Ceramic Veneers

Lab made

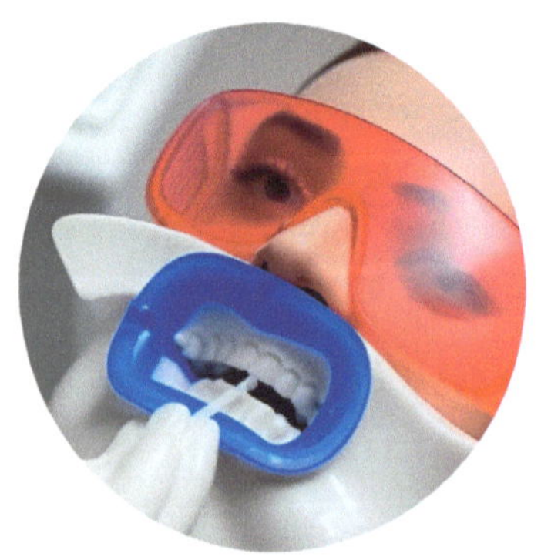

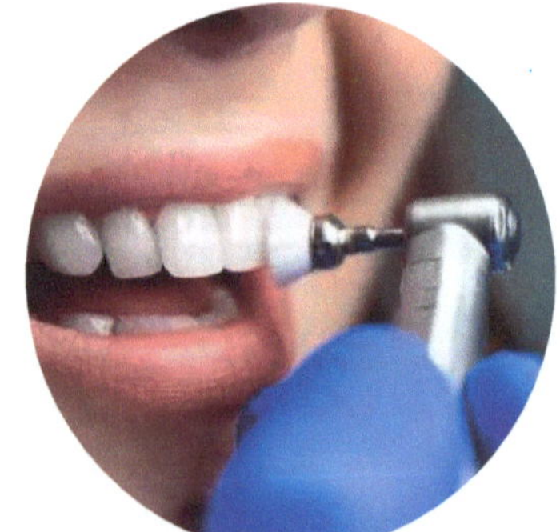

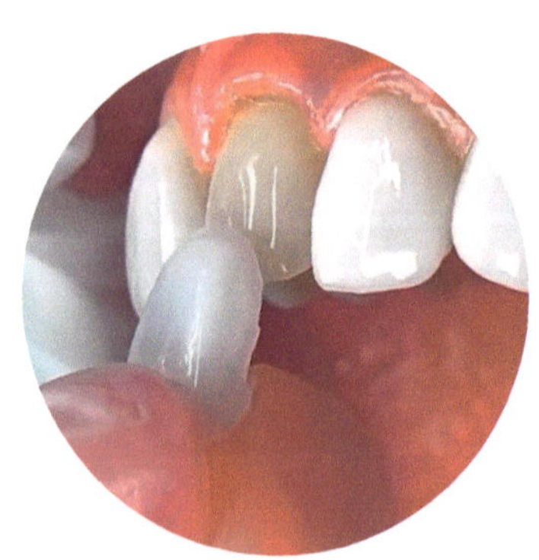

VENEERS

DIRECT-COMPOSITE
INDIRECT-COMPOSITE-LABMADE
LITHIUM DISILICATE-EMAX

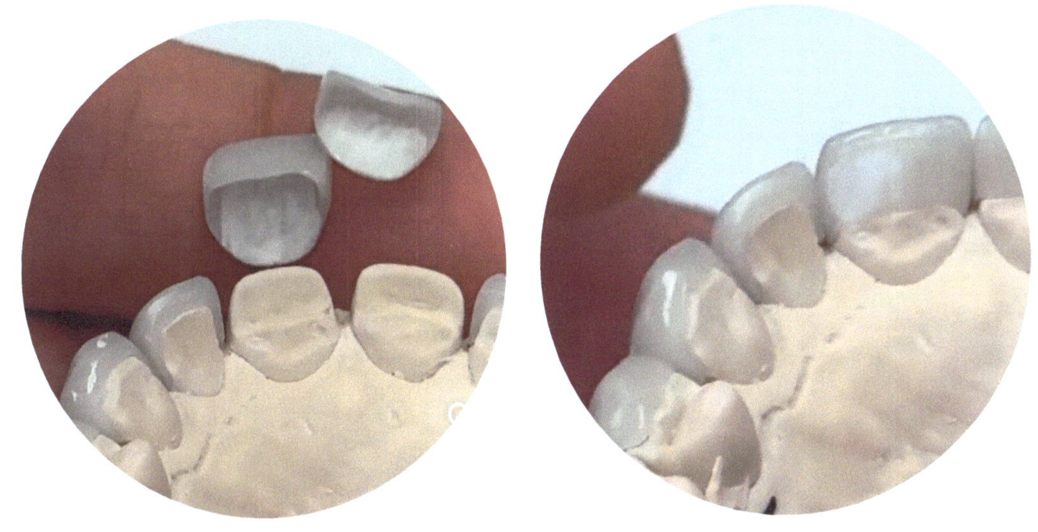

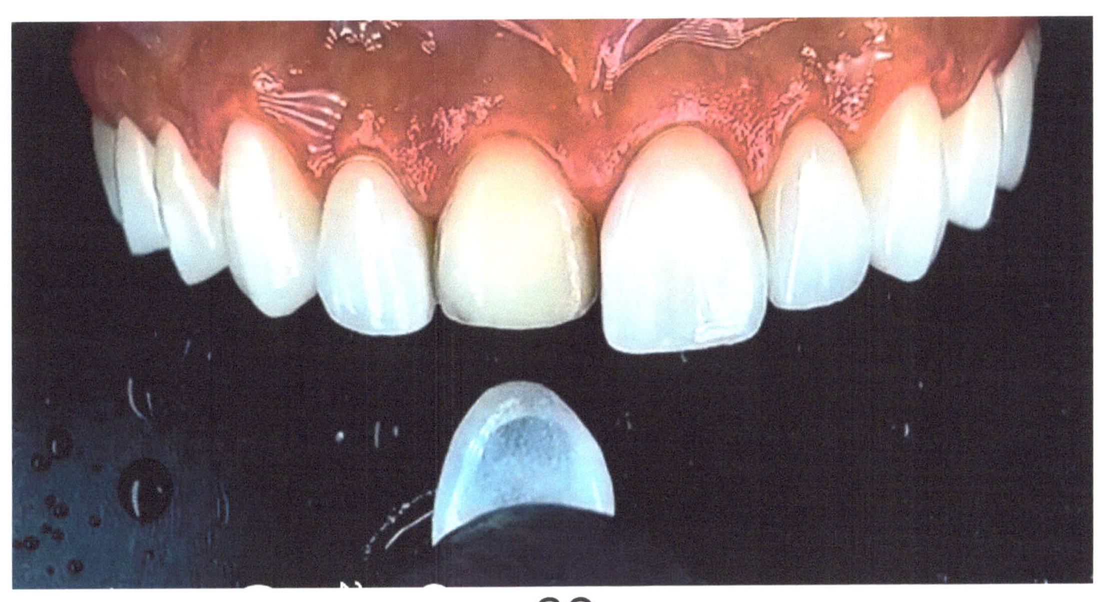

COMPOSITE
DIRECT-COMPOSITE

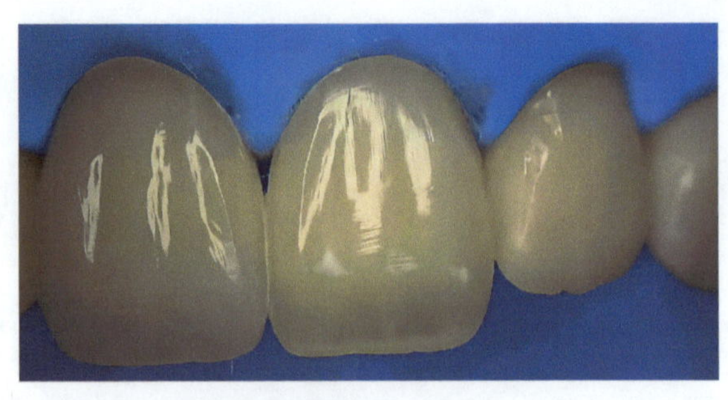

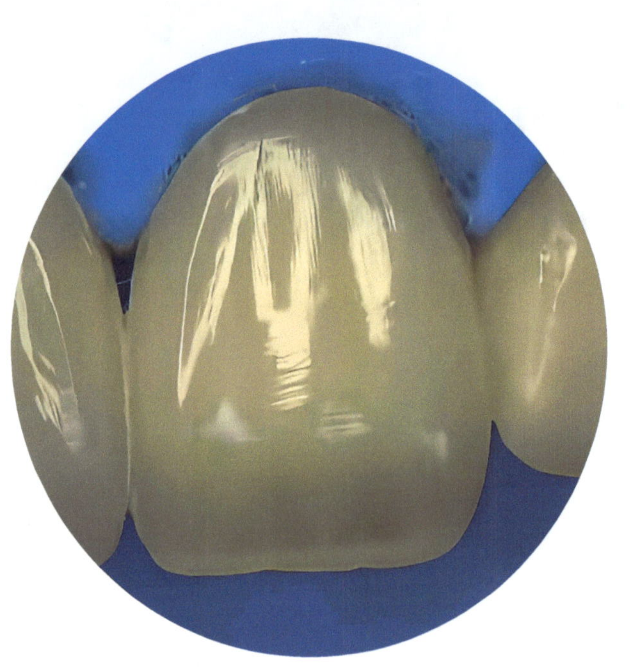

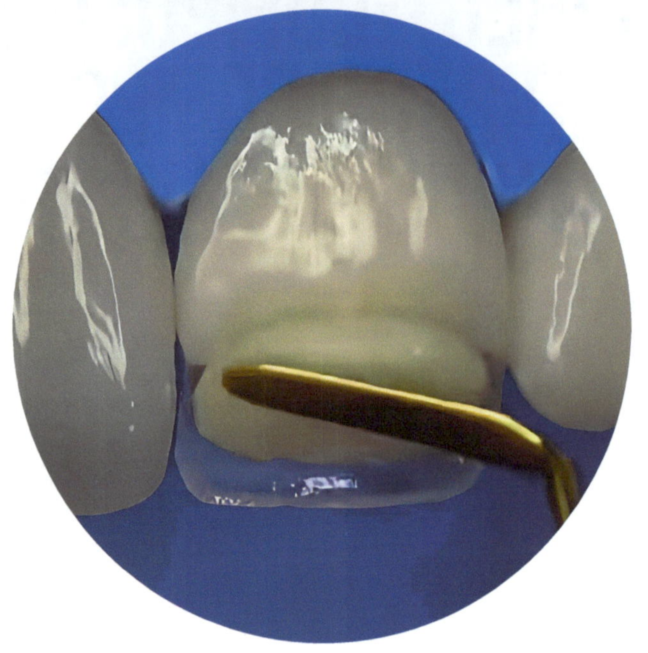

BRIDGE VS IMPLANT

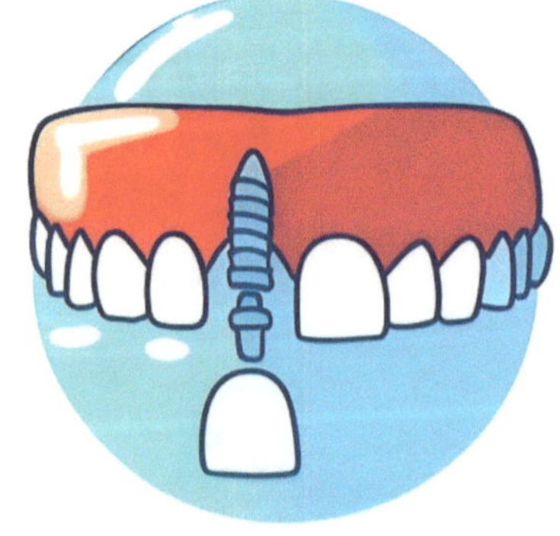

SEMI FIX PROSTHESIS

IMPLANT ALTERNATIVE FOR PERTICULAR SITUATION

TOOTH PREPRATION FOR SUPPORTING TEETH REQUIRED

PRECISION ATTACHMENT

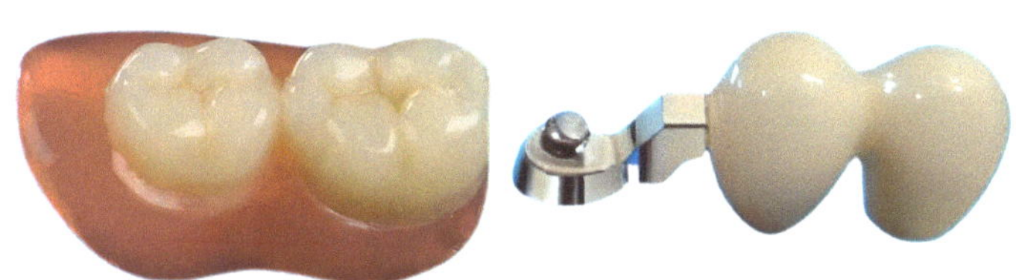

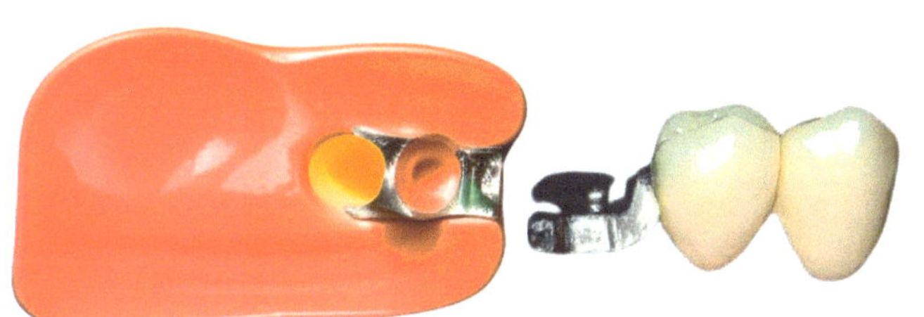

MERYLAND BRIDGE

PARTIAL SUPPORT FROM BACK
SIDE OF TRIMMED SURFACE

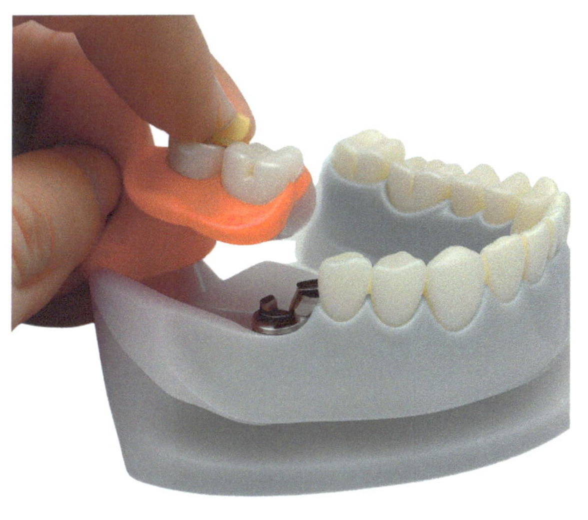

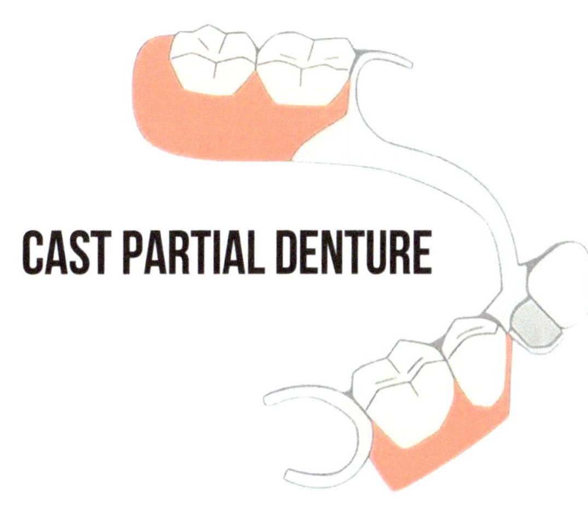

CAST PARTIAL DENTURE

REMOVABLE DENTURES
PATIENT CAN REMOVE DENTURE COMPLETE OR PARTIAL

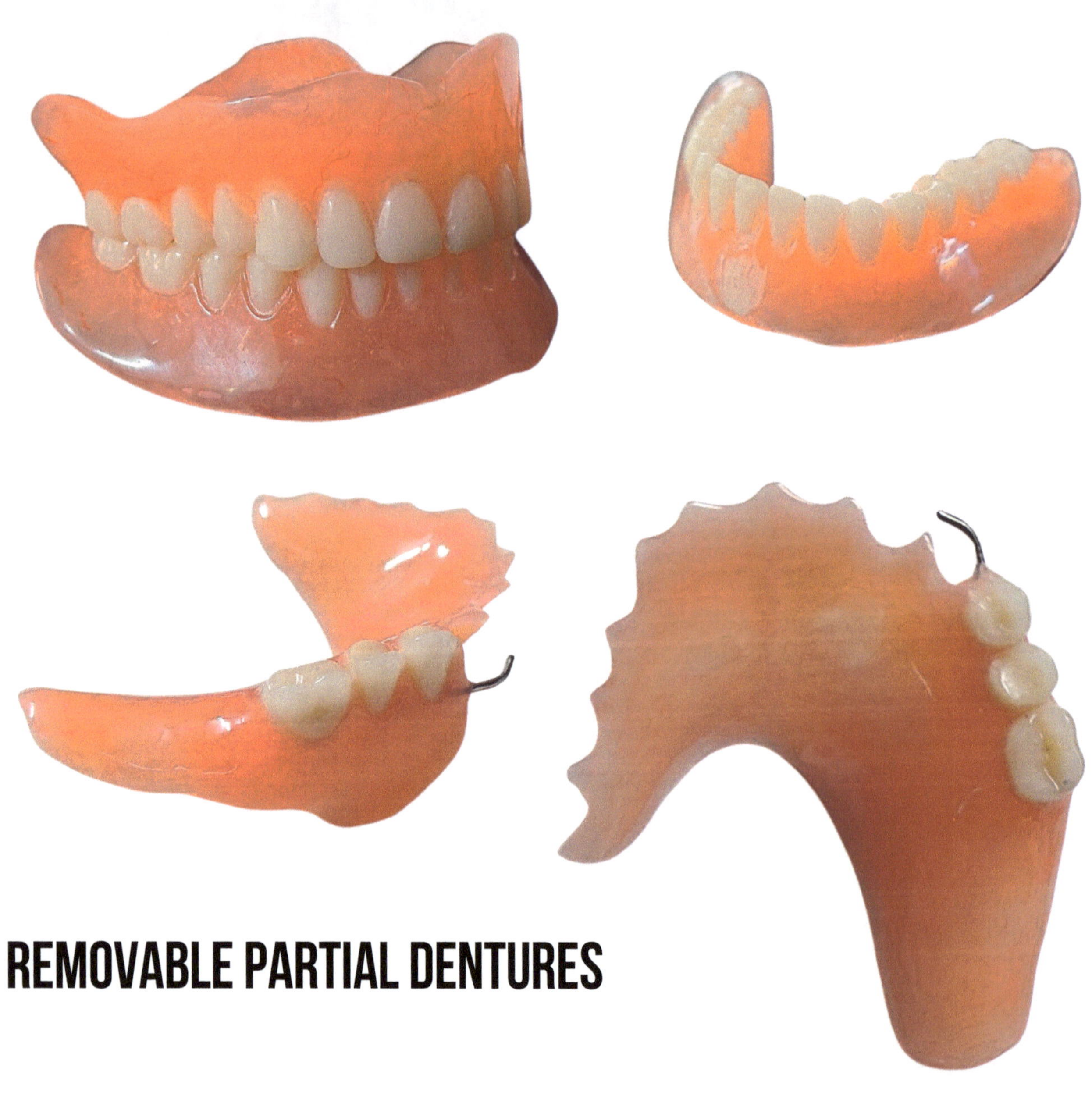

REMOVABLE PARTIAL DENTURES

IMPORTANCE OF PRIMARY TEETH (MILK TEETH)

- HEALTHY BABY TEETH LEAD TO HEALTHY ADULT TEETH!
- DON'T IGNORE MILK TEETH—STRONG FOUNDATIONS FOR LIFELONG SMILES.
- PROPER CARE FOR BABY TEETH HELPS AVOID FUTURE DENTAL ISSUES.

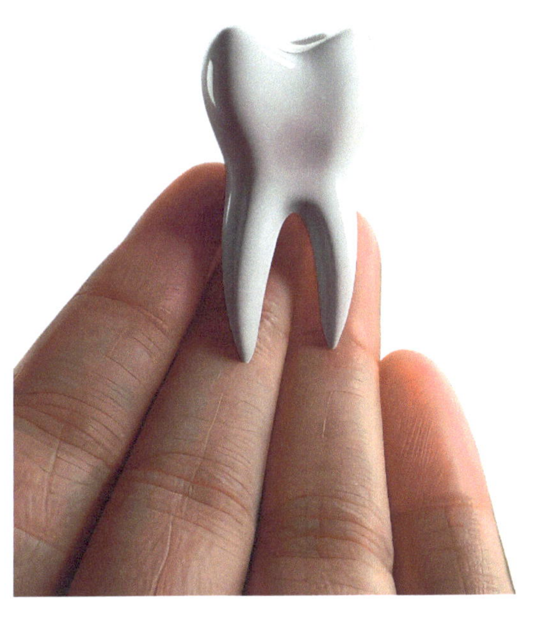

HEALTHY BABY TEETH HEALTHY FUTURE

BRUSHING TECHNIQUES FOR KIDS

- BRUSH TWICE A DAY TO KEEP CAVITIES AWAY!
- MAKE BRUSHING FUN—USE A TIMER OR A SONG FOR TWO MINUTES!
- PARENTS, HELP YOUR LITTLE ONES BRUSH UNTIL THEY CAN DO IT WELL THEMSELVES.

MAKE BRUSHING FUN!

COMMON TOOTHBRUSHING MISTAKES AND HOW TO AVOID THEM

1. Keeping Your Toothbrush for Too Long

The average toothbrush lasts only 3-4 months before the bristles become frayed and ineffective. Make it a habit to replace your toothbrush with the change of each season. Frayed bristles can't clean your teeth properly and might harm your gums. When buying a new toothbrush, look for one that meets globally accepted dental standards for quality and safety.

2. Not Brushing Long Enough

Many people don't brush their teeth for the recommended two minutes twice a day. In fact, most spend just 45 seconds brushing. To ensure thorough cleaning, set a timer or hum your favorite song that lasts about two minutes. Give your teeth the attention they deserve!

3. Brushing Too Hard

Gentle brushing is more effective than applying too much pressure. Brushing too hard can wear down enamel, the protective layer on your teeth, and irritate your gums. Use light pressure and let your toothbrush do the work.

4. Brushing Right After Eating

If you feel the need to brush after eating or drinking, especially acidic foods like citrus fruits or soda, wait at least 30 minutes. Brushing immediately can damage enamel softened by acids. In the meantime, rinse your mouth with water or chew sugar-free gum to freshen up.

5. Storing Your Toothbrush Improperly

After brushing, store your toothbrush upright in an open area to let it air dry. Avoid keeping it in closed containers, where moisture can encourage germ growth. If your toothbrush is stored in a holder with others, make sure they don't touch to avoid cross-contamination.

6. Using a Brush with Hard Bristles

Always opt for a toothbrush with soft bristles. Medium or hard bristles can erode enamel and cause tooth sensitivity, especially to cold food or drinks. Soft bristles effectively clean your teeth while being gentle on your gums.

7. Improper Brushing Technique

Master the right brushing technique:

- Place your toothbrush at a 45-degree angle to the gums.
- Move the brush gently back and forth in short strokes that cover the width of your teeth.
- Brush the outer, inner, and chewing surfaces of all teeth.
- To clean the inside surfaces of front teeth, tilt the brush vertically and use up-and-down strokes.

By following these tips and correcting common mistakes, you can maintain healthier teeth and gums for a lifetime.

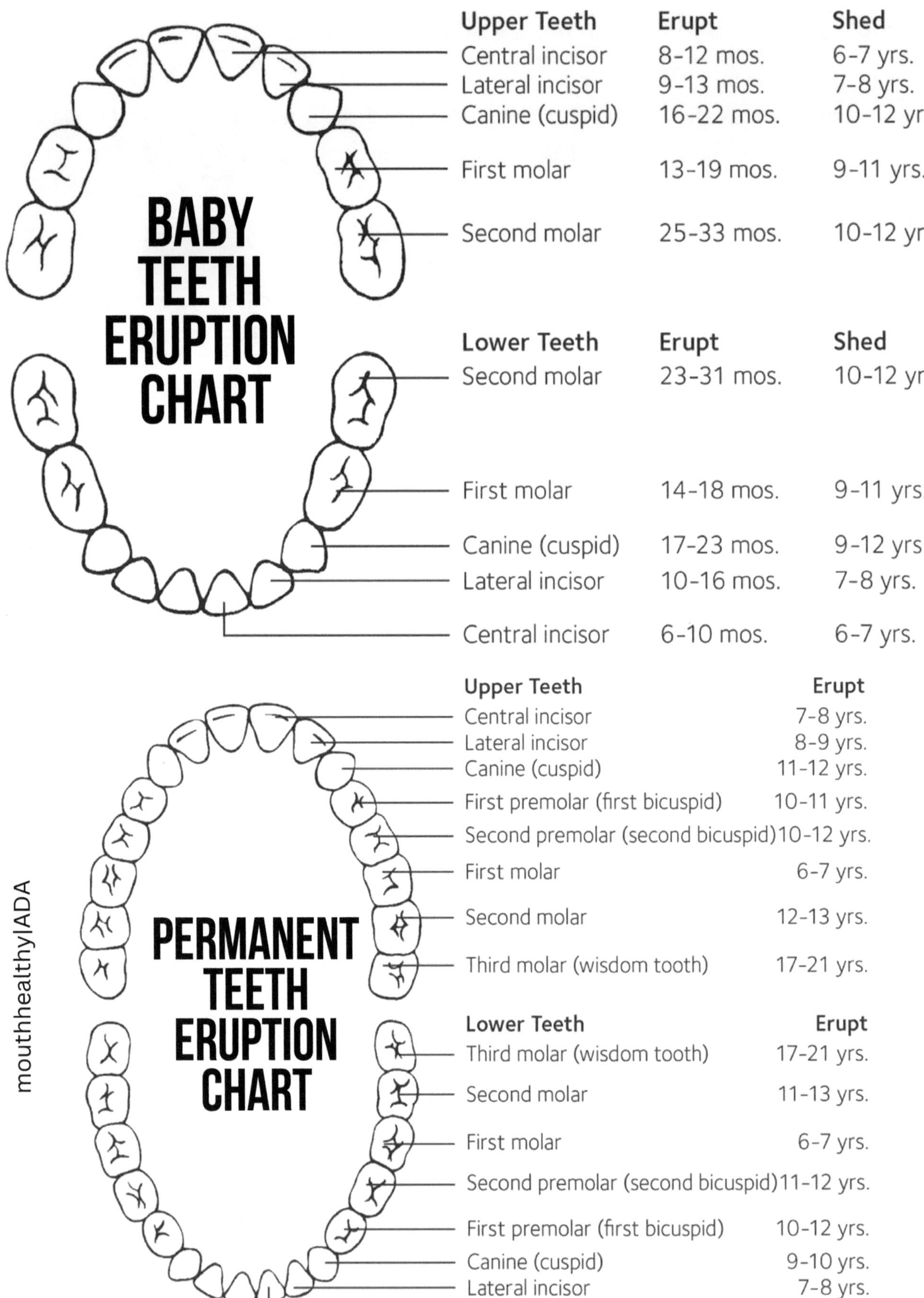
BABY TEETH ERUPTION CHART
Upper Teeth	Erupt	Shed
Central incisor	8-12 mos.	6-7 yrs.
Lateral incisor	9-13 mos.	7-8 yrs.
Canine (cuspid)	16-22 mos.	10-12 yrs.
First molar	13-19 mos.	9-11 yrs.
Second molar	25-33 mos.	10-12 yrs.
Lower Teeth	Erupt	Shed
Second molar	23-31 mos.	10-12 yrs.
First molar	14-18 mos.	9-11 yrs.
Canine (cuspid)	17-23 mos.	9-12 yrs.
Lateral incisor	10-16 mos.	7-8 yrs.
Central incisor	6-10 mos.	6-7 yrs.
PERMANENT TEETH ERUPTION CHART
Upper Teeth	Erupt
Central incisor	7-8 yrs.
Lateral incisor	8-9 yrs.
Canine (cuspid)	11-12 yrs.
First premolar (first bicuspid)	10-11 yrs.
Second premolar (second bicuspid)	10-12 yrs.
First molar	6-7 yrs.
Second molar	12-13 yrs.
Third molar (wisdom tooth)	17-21 yrs.
Lower Teeth	Erupt
Third molar (wisdom tooth)	17-21 yrs.
Second molar	11-13 yrs.
First molar	6-7 yrs.
Second premolar (second bicuspid)	11-12 yrs.
First premolar (first bicuspid)	10-12 yrs.
Canine (cuspid)	9-10 yrs.
Lateral incisor	7-8 yrs.
Central incisor	6-7 yrs.
mouthhealthy|ADA

PREVENTIVE DENTAL CARE: A KEY TO LIFELONG ORAL HEALTH

1. Importance of Preventive Care
   - Preventive dental care helps avoid cavities, gum disease, enamel wear, and other oral health problems.
   - It is cost-effective and ensures early detection of potential issues.
2. Daily Oral Hygiene Practices
   - Brushing: Brush twice a day using fluoride toothpaste and a soft-bristled toothbrush.
   - Flossing: Clean between teeth daily to remove food particles and plaque.
   - Mouthwash: Use an antimicrobial mouth rinse to reduce bacteria.
3. Balanced Diet for Healthy Teeth
   - Eat a diet rich in fruits, vegetables, whole grains, and lean proteins.
   - Limit sugary snacks and beverages, as they contribute to tooth decay.
4. Regular Dental Checkups
   - Visit the dentist at least twice a year for professional cleanings and exams.
   - Early diagnosis of issues like cavities, gum disease, and oral cancer is crucial.
5. Protective Measures
   - Use a mouthguard during sports activities to prevent injuries.
   - Consider dental sealants for children to protect the chewing surfaces of molars.
6. Fluoride Benefits
   - Fluoride strengthens tooth enamel and makes it more resistant to decay.
   - Incorporate fluoridated water or professional fluoride treatments as recommended.
7. Special Care for High-Risk Patients
   - Patients with diabetes, smokers, or pregnant women may need personalized care plans.
   - Children and older adults may also require specific preventive measures.
8. Preventing Common Dental Issues
   - Cavities: Maintain good oral hygiene and dietary habits.
   - Gum Disease: Control plaque buildup and treat early symptoms like bleeding gums.
   - Tooth Sensitivity: Use toothpaste for sensitive teeth and avoid acidic foods.
9. Role of Education
   - Teach patients about the impact of oral health on overall well-being.
10. Innovative Tools for Prevention
   - Electric toothbrushes, interdental brushes, and water flossers can enhance oral care routines.
   - Emphasize the role of technology like AI-powered dental apps in tracking oral health.

PREVENTIVE CARE
PRODUCTS

Mouthwash

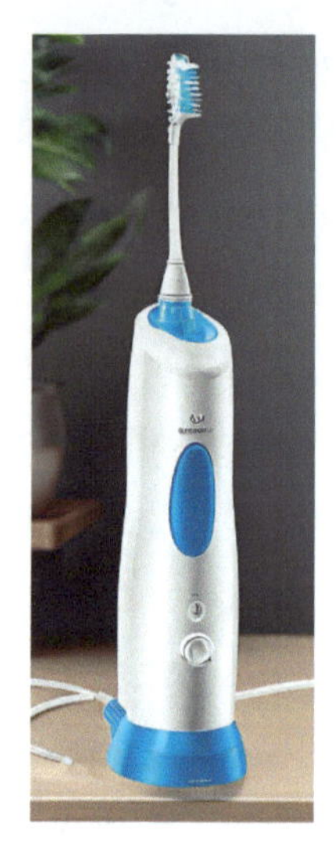

Waterflosser

Electric Brush

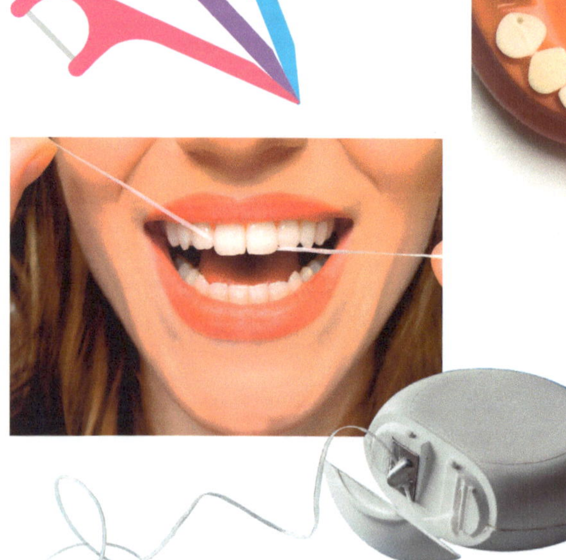

Thread floss

Inter Dental Brush

MOUTH IS GATEWAY OF BODY, KEEP ENTRANCE CLEAN

IMPACT OF ORAL HEALTH ON GENERAL HEALTH

1. Oral-Systemic Connections

- Cardiovascular Disease: Gum disease (periodontitis) increases the risk of heart disease due to chronic inflammation and bacteria entering the bloodstream.
- Diabetes: Poorly managed diabetes can worsen gum disease, and severe gum disease can make diabetes harder to control.
- Respiratory Infections: Bacteria from oral infections can be inhaled into the lungs, leading to pneumonia or worsening existing respiratory conditions.
- Pregnancy Complications: Periodontal disease is linked to premature birth and low birth weight.
- Osteoporosis: Bone loss in the jaw due to advanced gum disease mirrors the loss seen in osteoporosis.
- Alzheimer's Disease: Studies suggest chronic gum inflammation may increase the risk of cognitive decline.

2. Nutritional Impact

- Poor oral health can make chewing difficult, leading to inadequate nutrition.
- Missing teeth or oral pain can result in reliance on soft, less nutritious foods.

3. Inflammation and Immune Response

- Chronic oral infections contribute to systemic inflammation, which can worsen conditions like arthritis and cardiovascular disease.

4. Psychological Impact

- Oral health issues can affect self-esteem, social interactions, and mental health, contributing to conditions like depression or anxiety.

5. Preventive Measures

- Maintaining good oral hygiene reduces the risk of systemic diseases.
- Regular dental visits aid in early detection and prevention of complications.

DENTAL PROBLEMS MAY AFFECT THE HEART HEALTH

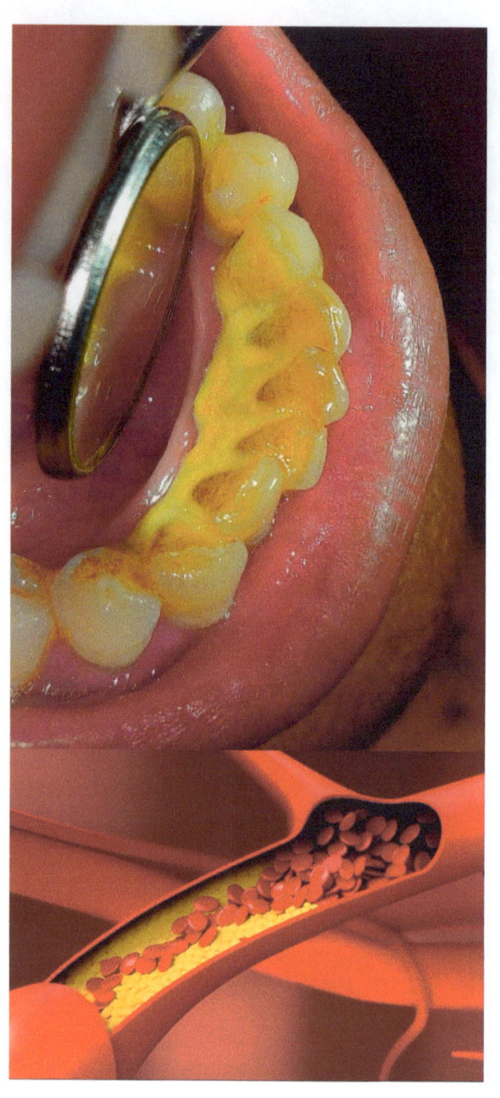

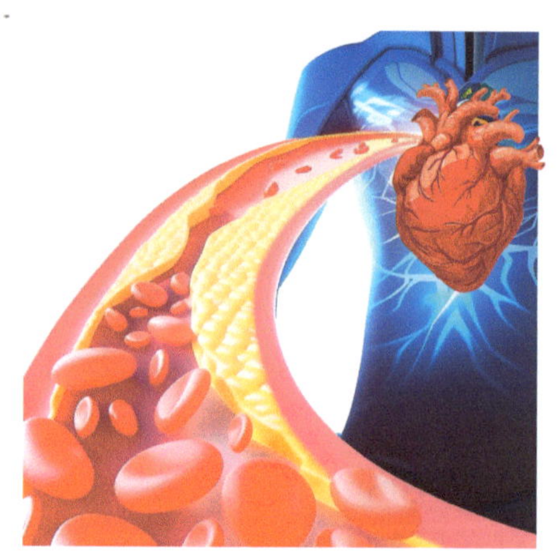

Dental health is crucial during pregnancy as hormonal changes can increase the risk of gum disease and tooth decay. Regular dental checkups and good oral hygiene help prevent complications like pregnancy gingivitis. Avoid skipping dental treatments; they are safe and essential for both mother and baby. A healthy smile supports a healthy pregnancy!

PULPOTOMY

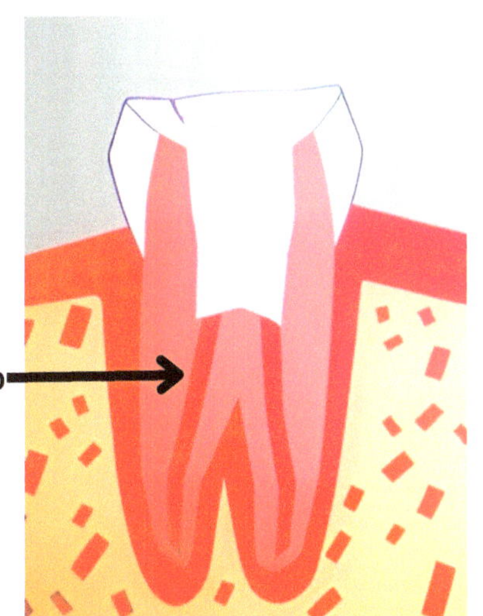

- Dental procedure removing infected coronal pulp while preserving vital roots.
- Indication: Primary teeth with pulp exposure, irreversible inflammation, or caries.
- Benefits: Relieves pain, preserves tooth, maintains function, prevents extraction.

PULPECTOMY

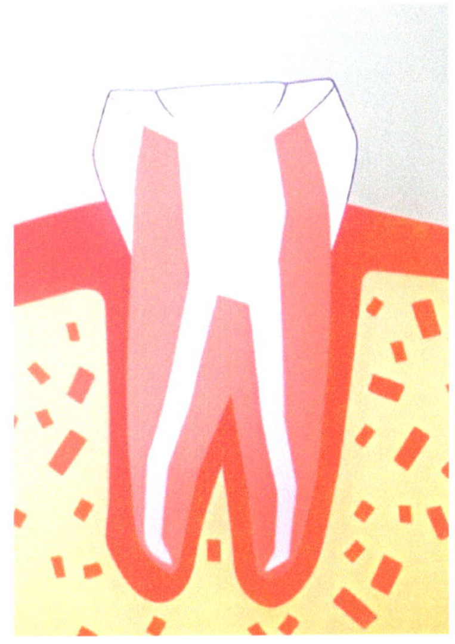

- Complete removal of pulp from root canals in teeth.
- Indication: Severely infected, necrotic pulp in primary or young teeth.
- Benefits: Eliminates infection, maintains tooth space, restores chewing functionality.

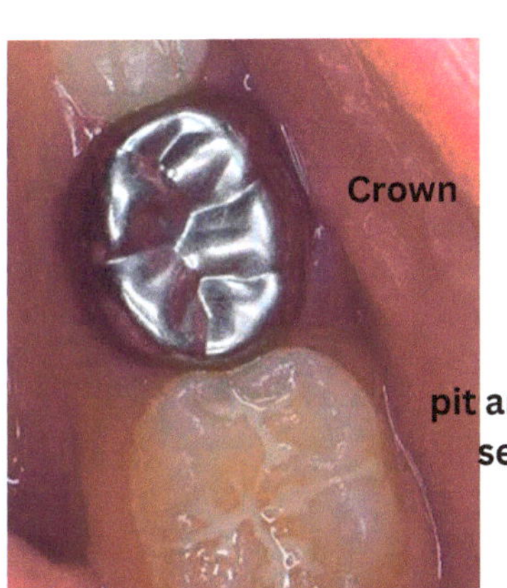

- Definition: Prefabricated crowns restoring decayed, damaged, or treated primary teeth.
- Indication: Extensive caries, pulpotomy, pulpectomy, fractured teeth, or enamel defects.
- Benefits: Durable, cost-effective, protects tooth, maintains function and alignment.

HABBITS
HABBIT BREAKING DEVICES

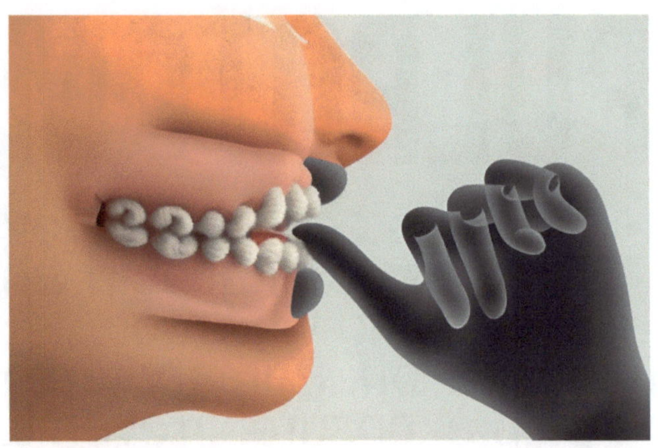

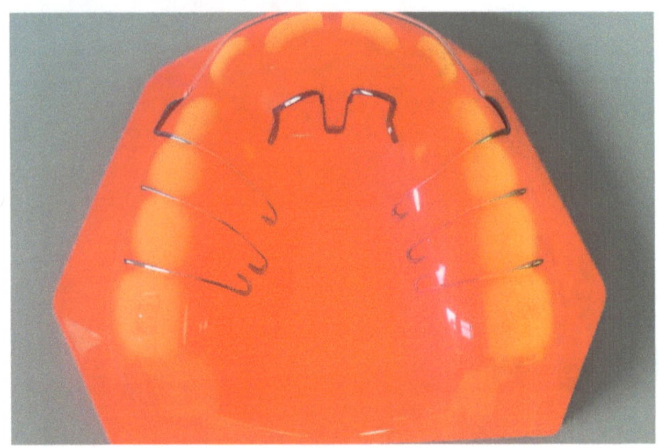

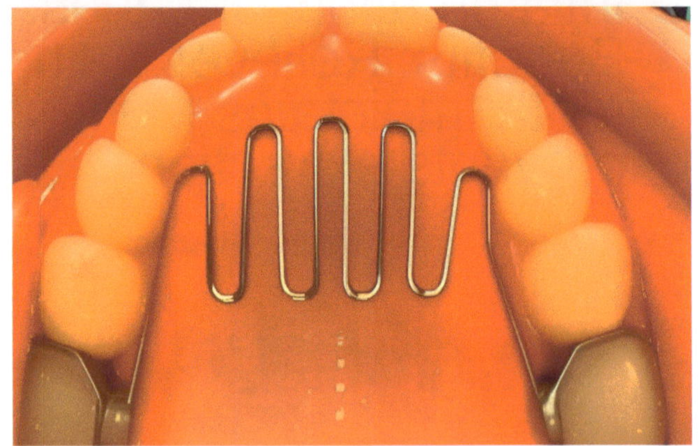

DEVICES PREVENTS HARMFUL HABITS LIKE THUMB-SUCKING OR TONGUE-THRUSTING.

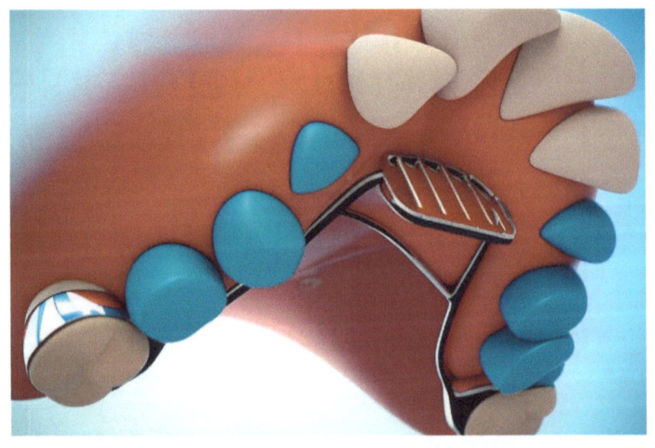

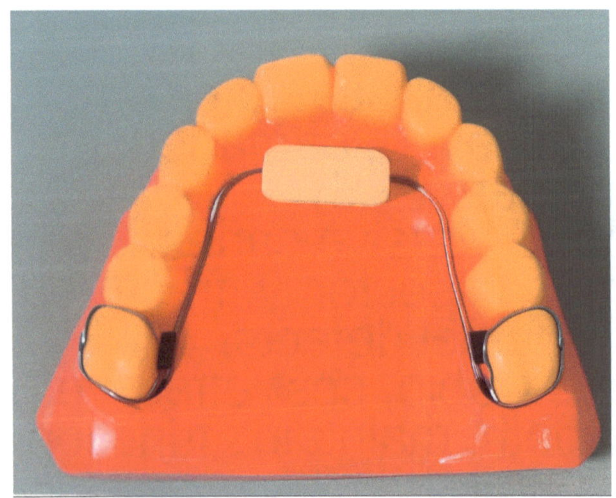

- TYPES: FIXED APPLIANCES, REMOVABLE APPLIANCES, CUSTOM-MADE DESIGNS AVAILABLE.
- BENEFITS: CORRECTS ORAL POSTURE, PREVENTS MALOCCLUSION, ENSURES HEALTHY GROWTH.

SPACE
MAINTAINERS

DEVICES PRESERVS SPACE AFTER PREMATURE LOSS OF PRIMARY TEETH.

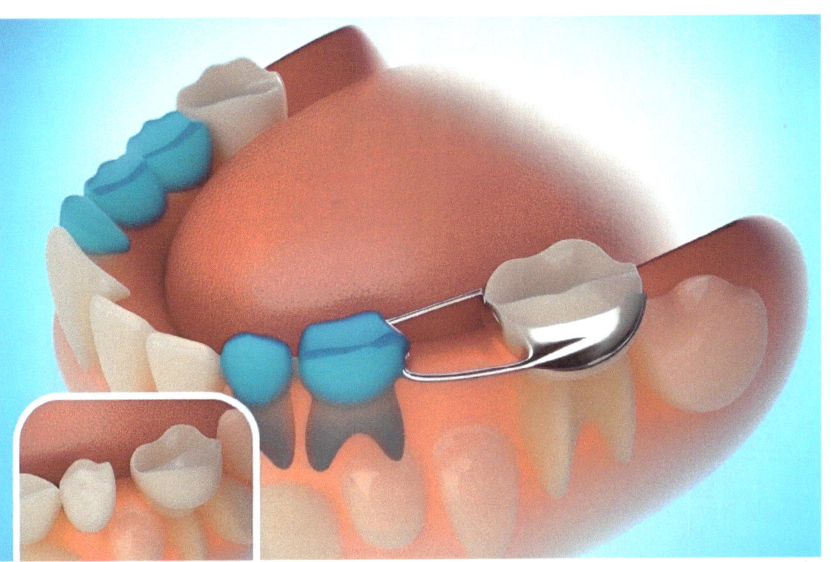

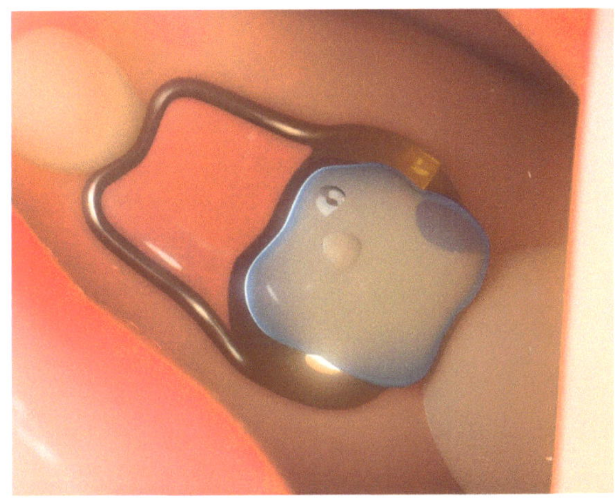

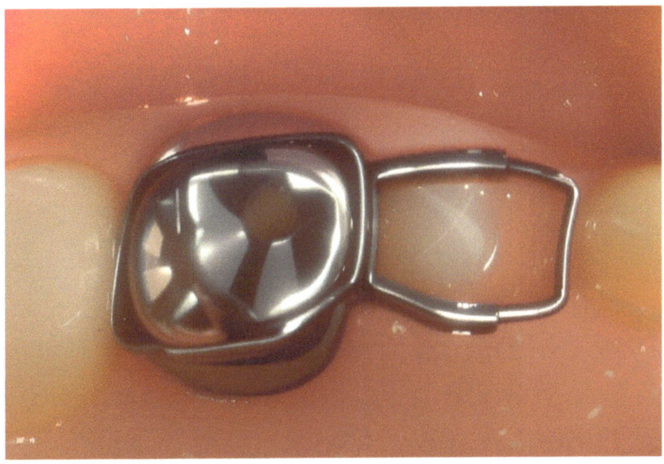

- TYPES: FIXED BAND-LOOP, CROWN-LOOP, AND REMOVABLE ACRYLIC OPTIONS.
- BENEFITS: PREVENTS CROWDING, AIDS ERUPTION, ENSURES PROPER DENTAL ALIGNMENT.

TRAUMA

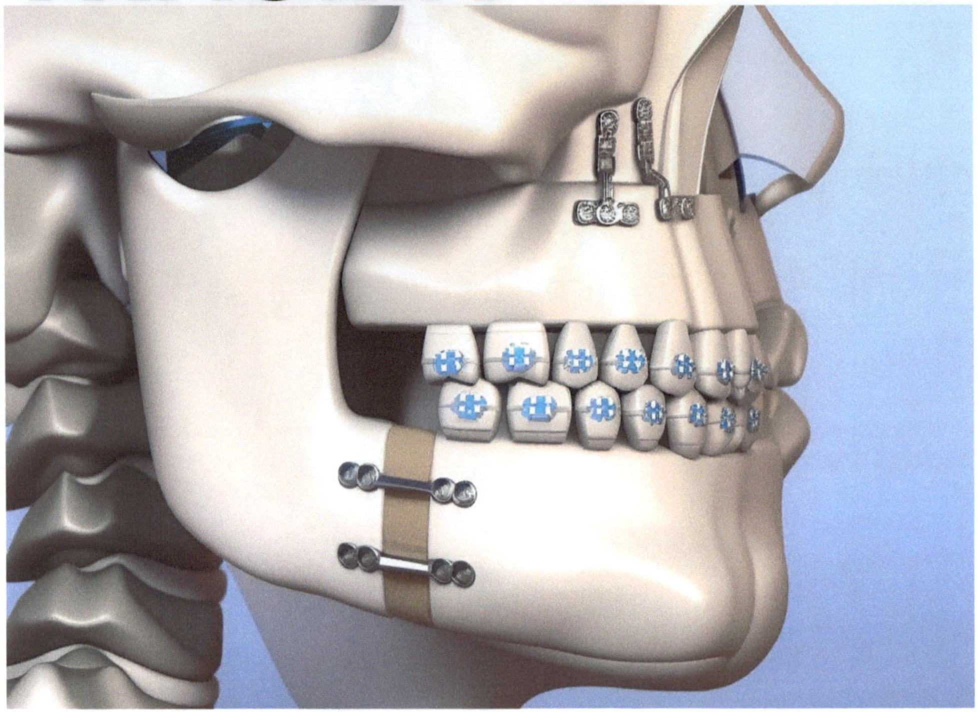

Types of Dental Trauma

1. Tooth fracture: A crack or break in the tooth structure.

2. Tooth luxation: A tooth that is partially or completely displaced from its socket.

3. Tooth avulsion: A tooth that is completely knocked out of its socket.

4. Dental concussion: A tooth that is tender to touch but has no visible signs of damage.

Causes of Dental Trauma

1. Sports injuries: Contact sports like football, hockey, and basketball.

2. Falls: Accidental falls or slips.

3. Car accidents: Trauma from airbags or steering wheels.

4. Assaults: Physical altercations.

Symptoms of Dental Trauma

1. Tooth pain: Sharp or dull pain in the affected tooth.

2. Tooth mobility: Loosening of the tooth.

3. Bleeding: Bleeding from the gums or tooth socket.

4. Swelling: Swelling of the face, gums, or lips.

Treatment of Dental Trauma

Airway, Breathing ,Cerculation and other general aspects are analysed

1. Emergency care: Immediate treatment to relieve pain and stabilize the tooth.
2. Root canal therapy: Treatment to save the tooth by removing infected pulp.
3. Tooth splinting: Stabilizing the tooth with a splint.
4. Tooth extraction: Removing the tooth if it's beyond repair.

ATTRISION

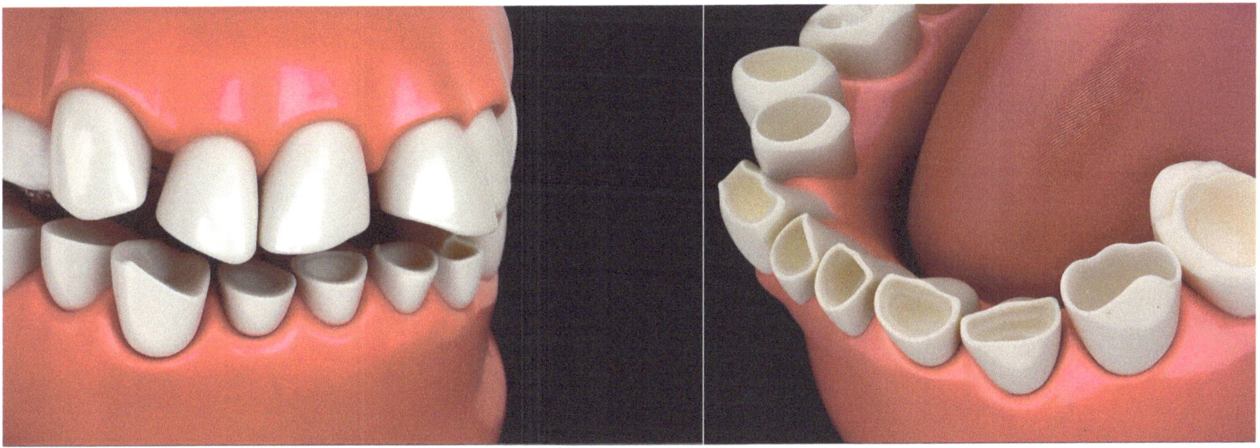

Dental attrition is the gradual loss of tooth structure due to tooth-to-tooth contact, often caused by grinding or clenching over time. It can lead to flattened tooth surfaces, sensitivity, and compromised oral function.

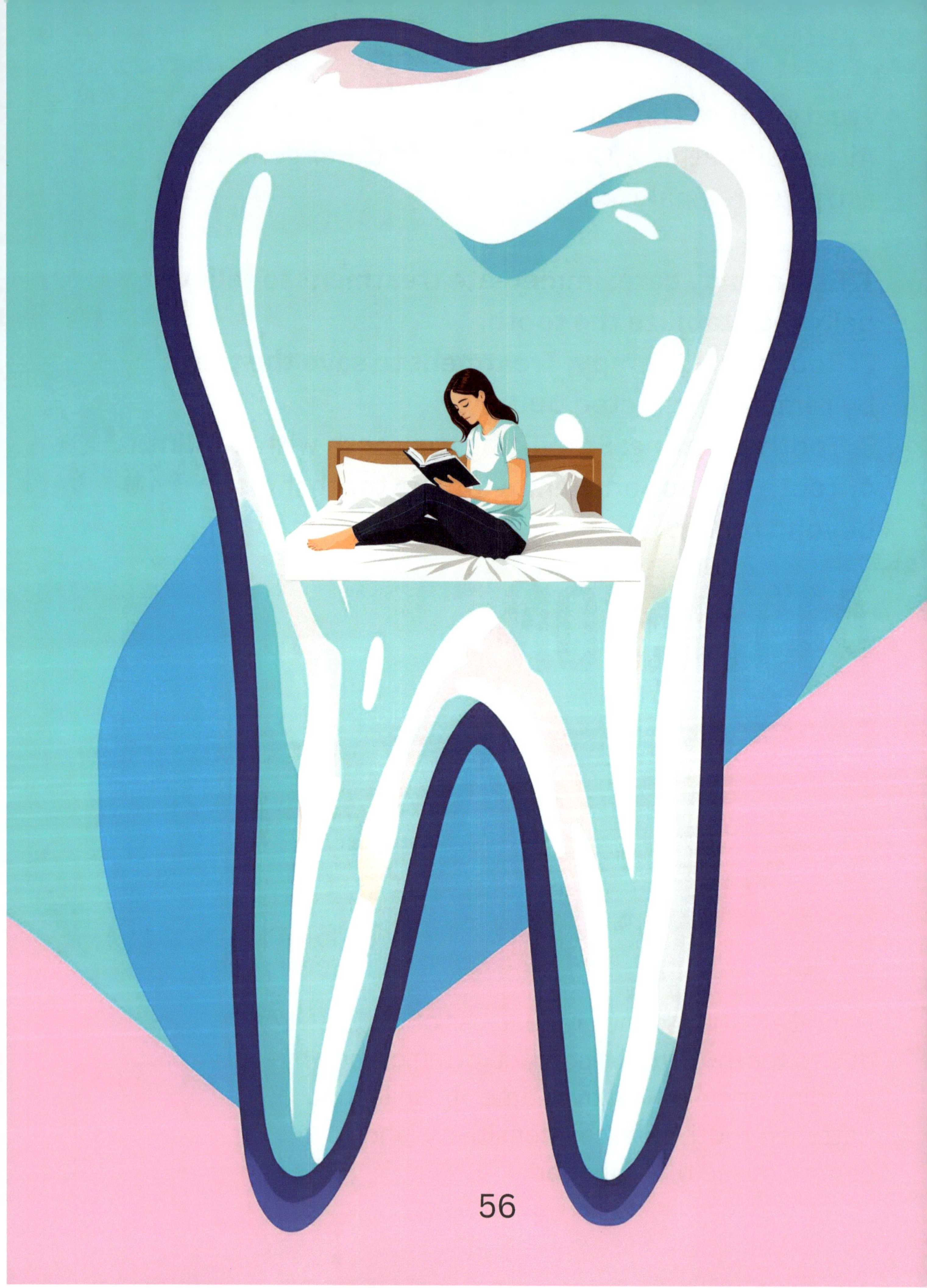

CARIES SPREAD FROM MARGIN
WITHOUT PAIN

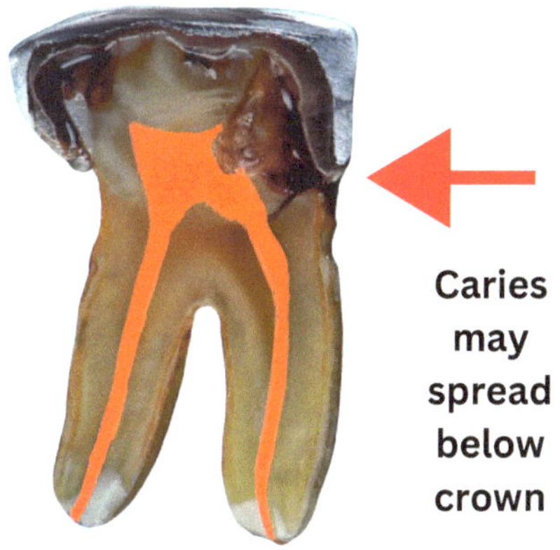

Caries may spread below crown

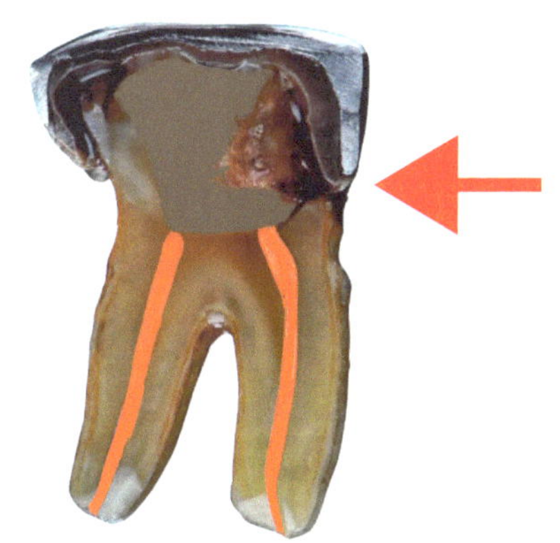

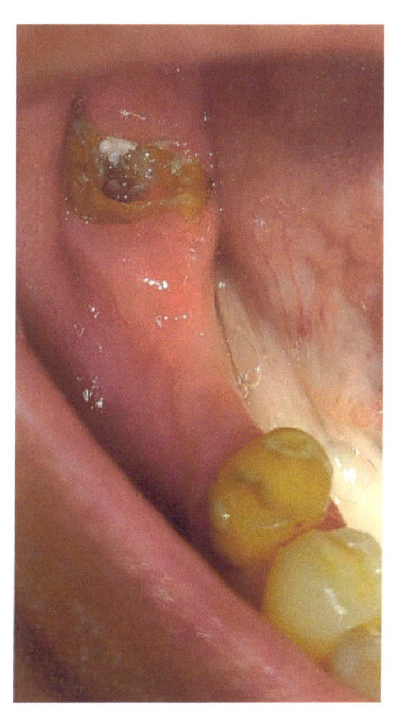

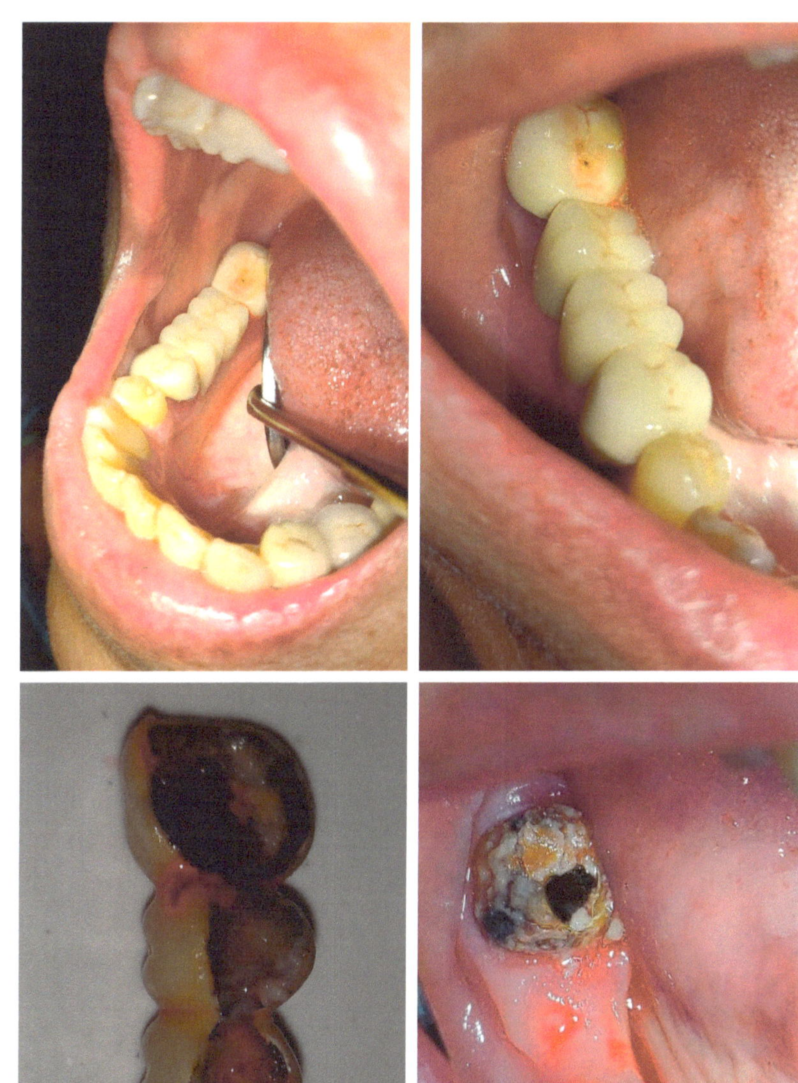

AFTER OPENING BRIDGE/CROWN

REMEMBER NOTHING IS PERMENANT IN THIS WORLD, YES! SOMETHING CANBE

LONGLASTING IF TIMELY TAKEN CARE, SERVICES,MAINTAINANCE MATTERS A LOT

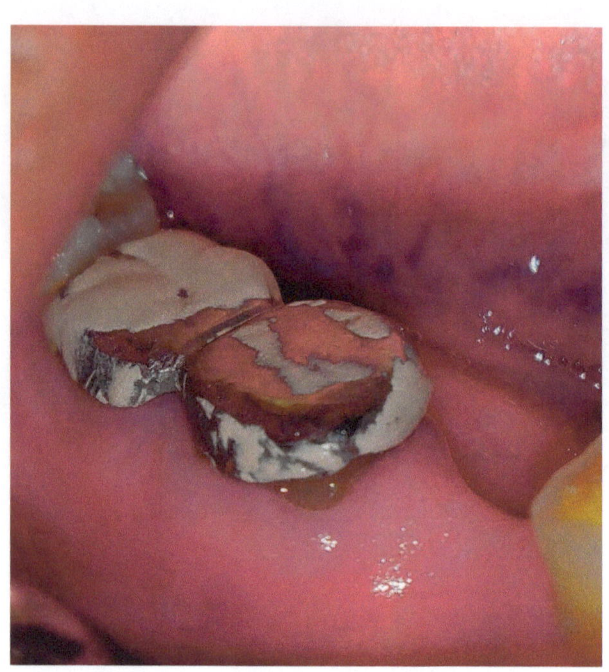

CROWN CAN CHIP, CRACK, OR EVEN BREAK.

IN ANY CASE, A CROWN IS DESIGNED TO WITHSTAND THE PRESSURE OF CHEWING, ALLOWING YOU TO USE YOUR RESTORED TOOTH JUST LIKE YOU DO YOUR NATURAL TEETH. AND JUST LIKE NATURAL TEETH, A DENTAL CROWN CAN CHIP, CRACK, OR EVEN BREAK.

EXCESSIVE BITINGFORCE , SINGLE SIDE CHEWING, OCCLUSION,FABRICATION OF CROWN ETC REASONS OF CERAMIC CHIP IN PFM CROWNS

THE NUMBER ONE REASON FOR DENTAL CAP KEEP COMING OFF IS LACK OF RETENTION, AND TOOTH STRUCTURE IS COMPROMISED TO HOLD THE DENTAL CAP. YOUR CROWN MUST HAVE ENOUGH RETENTION TO STAY ON THE TOOTH EVEN WITHOUT ANY CEMENT.

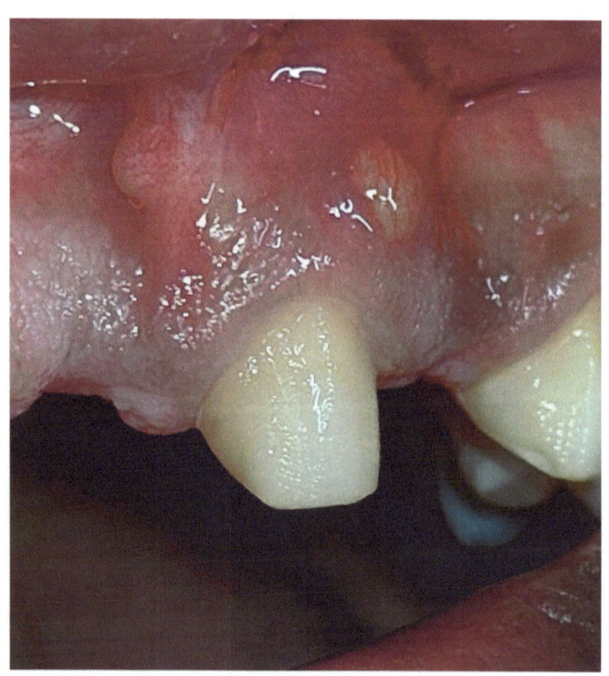

DENTAL INFECTION DUE TO PAST TRAUMA

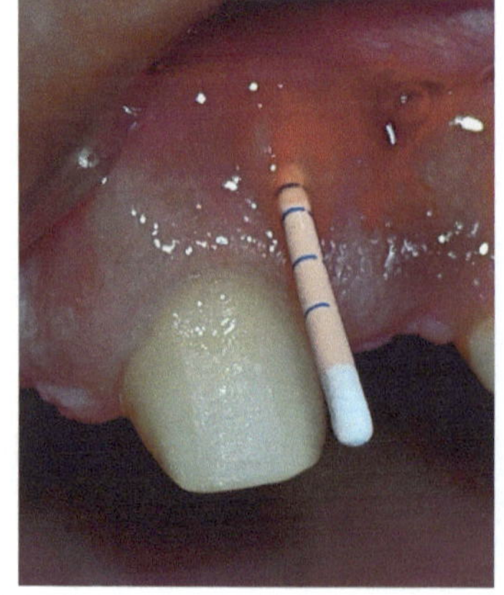

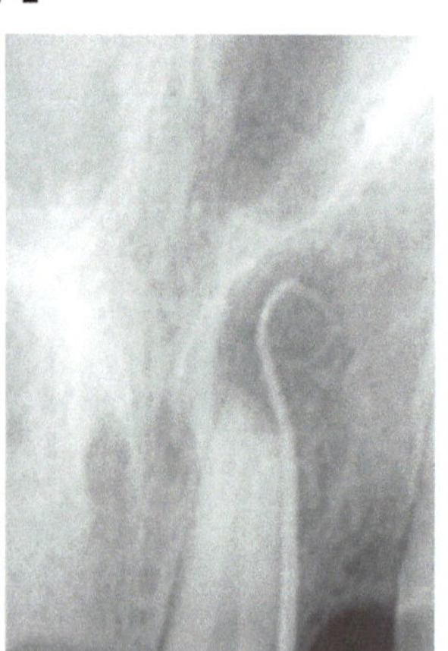

MINIMAL INVESIVE CONSERVATIVE BIOMIMETIC

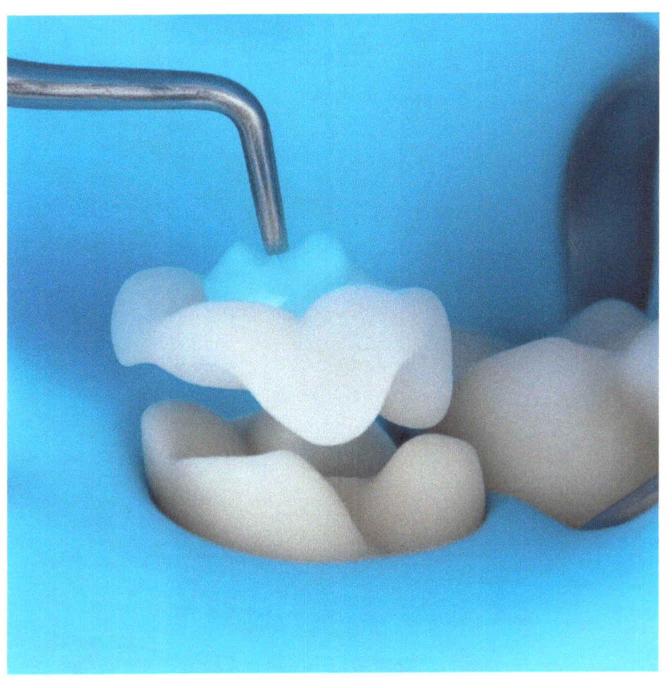

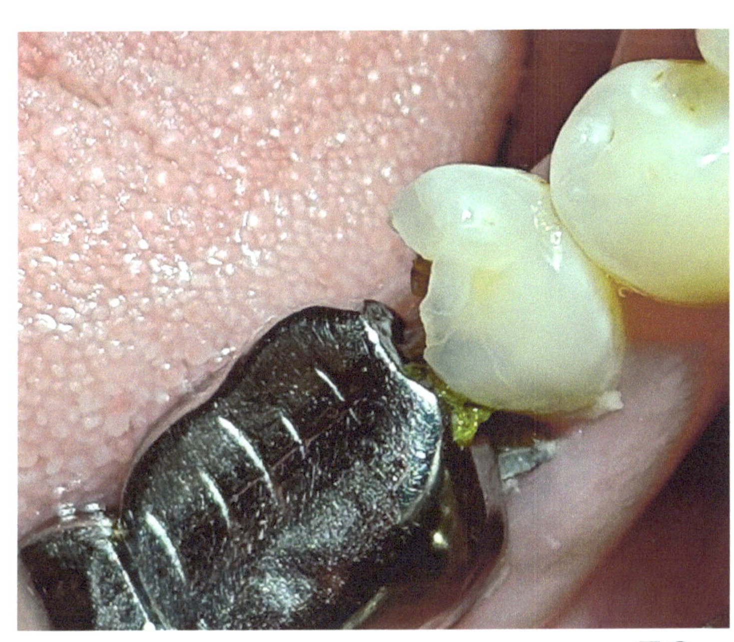

PROXIMAL CARIES

Dental & Skin Artworks

& Patient Education Posters available

At www.StatusRing.in

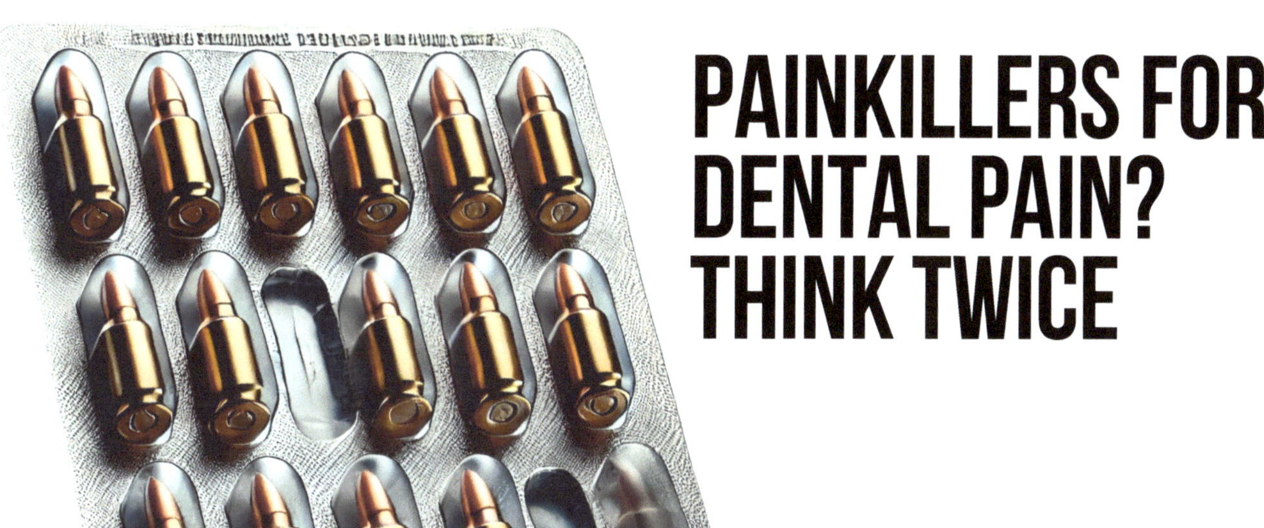

PAINKILLERS FOR DENTAL PAIN? THINK TWICE

Medicines are an essential part of managing dental conditions but are often a part of a comprehensive treatment plan rather than a standalone solution.

They provide temporary relief by alleviating pain, reducing swelling, or controlling infections, but they cannot address the root cause of many dental issues. For example, painkillers can ease discomfort, but they cannot cure cavities, sensitivity, or root canal infections.

Long-term oral health requires a combination of medication, professional dental care, proper hygiene practices, and timely interventions. Problems like cavities or infections need definitive treatments such as fillings, root canal therapy, or periodontal care. Always use dental medicines as prescribed by your dentist, and remember that they are a supportive measure, not a substitute for proper dental treatment.

YES, MEDICINE HAS POWER TO SUPPORT YOUR JOURNEY ALONG WITH JOURNEY OF TOOTH DECAY WITHOUT PAIN

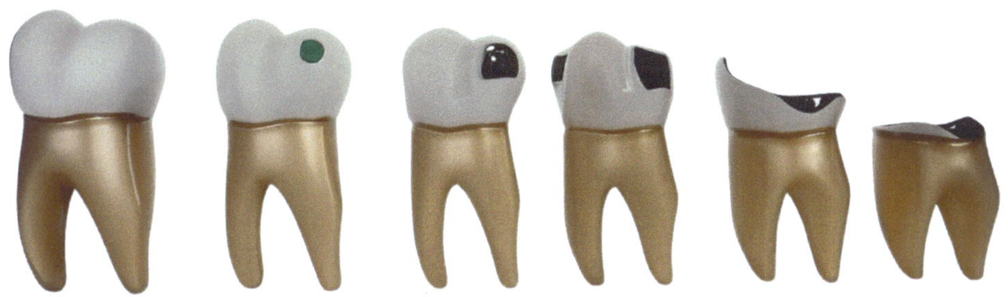

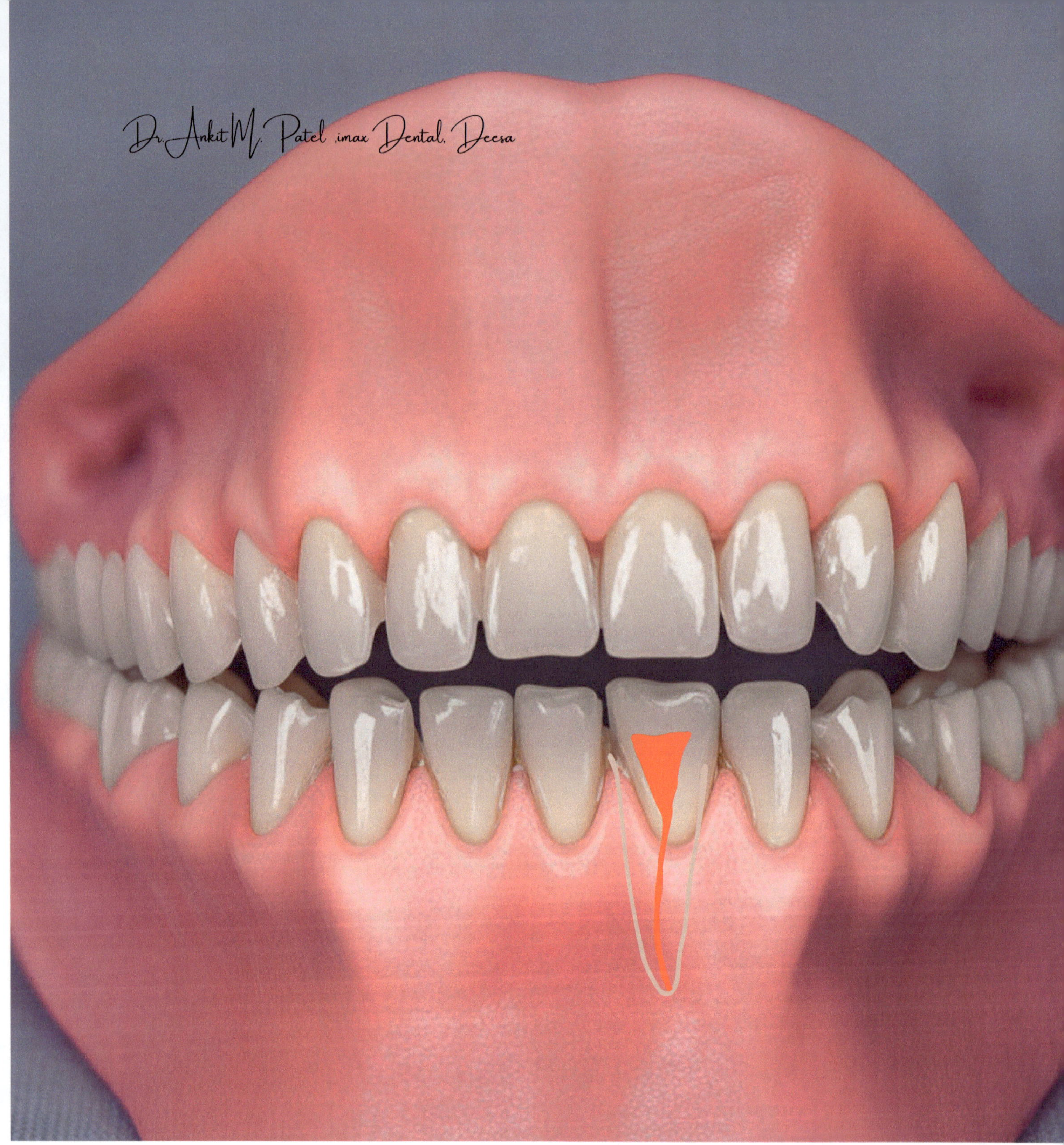

If you want to send comments, feedback,or want to suggest topics. Write us on thestatusring@gmail.com

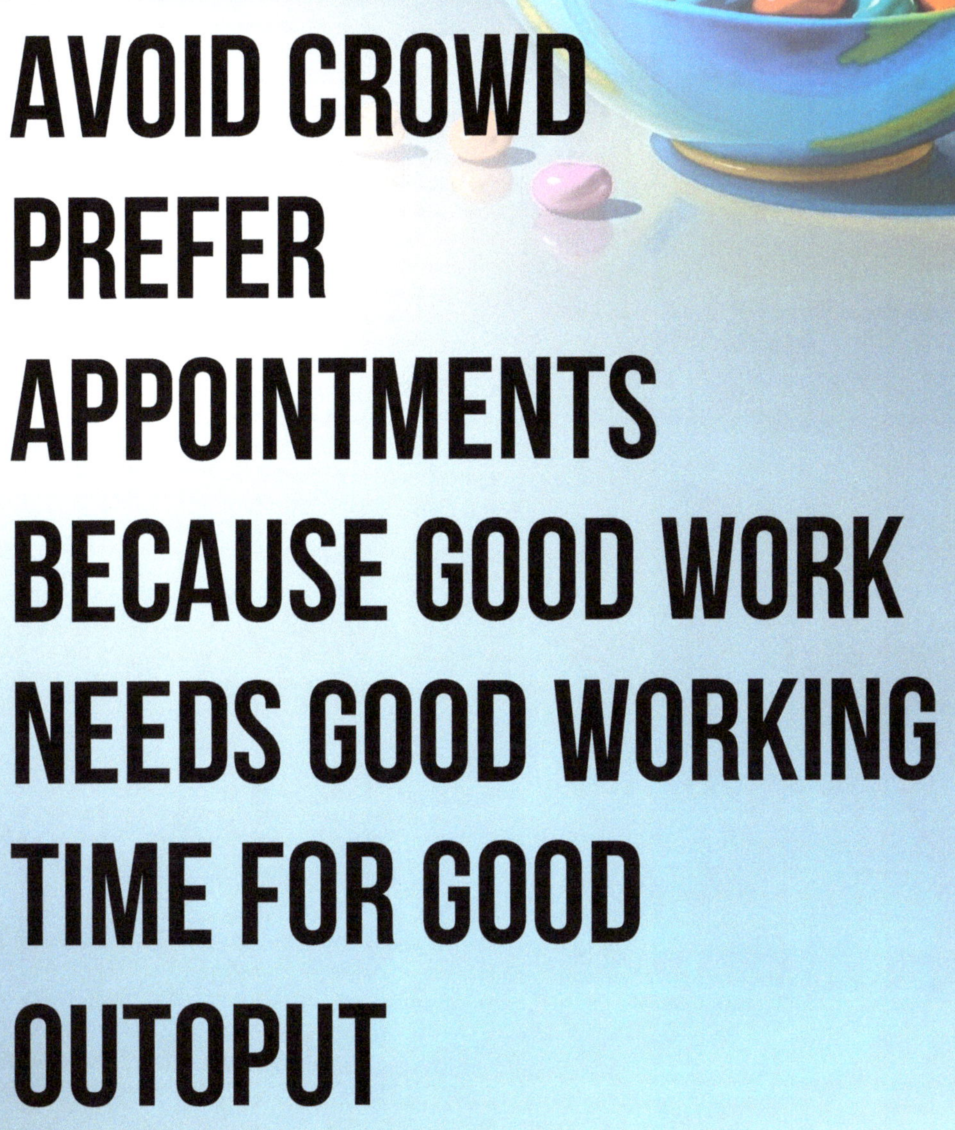

AVOID CROWD PREFER APPOINTMENTS BECAUSE GOOD WORK NEEDS GOOD WORKING TIME FOR GOOD OUTOPUT

NEVER MISS APPOINTMENT TIME INFORM EARLY IF YOU ARE NOT ABLE TO COME, SO OPERATOR CAN GIVE GOOD TIME TO OTHERS